With Inky Blots
and
Rotten Parchment

An Explanation of the
Land Value Tax

Ian Hopton

Grosvenor House
Publishing Limited

This book is published by
Grosvenor House Publishing Ltd
Link House
140 The Broadway, Tolworth, Surrey, KT6 7HT.
www.grosvenorhousepublishing.co.uk

A CIP record for this book
is available from the British Library

ISBN 978-1-83975-824-9
eBook ISBN 978-1-80381-133-8

CONTENTS

INTRODUCTION

The land, the earth God gave man for his home,
sustenance, and support, should never be the
possession of any man, corporation, society, or
unfriendly government, any more than the air or
water.

Abraham Lincoln (1809–65): 16th President of the US

The primary purpose of this book is to explain to
those with no particular knowledge of economics or
taxation the basic principles that lie behind land value
taxation, and why it may be seen as a fair and
appropriate way of raising revenue for local or central
government.

Economics is about the relationships that people have
within a society. It is usually associated with financial,
tax and business relationships, but there are many other
aspects involved: social, religious, marital and
generational considerations also play their part in the
economic settlement; how people live, work and play
together. Taxation, of course, plays a large part—how we
tax, what we tax, who we tax—all issues which are
endlessly debated and are often the source of much
disagreement. There are ways other than through

1

taxation by which governments may raise revenue, for instance through borrowing or simply by printing money, but these are secondary methods which are resorted to mainly in times of emergency. Taxation still remains the primary method and the proposition in this book is that a land value tax (LVT) would not only be a fair tax but also very effective in solving many of the problems that beset society at the present time, or in fact at any time.

Taxation is not a product of nature, it is a human invention, but it is arguably one of the most useful of all inventions. However, taxation has acquired a very bad name: It is seen by many as an evil, even though most would admit a necessary one, but this view is surely misguided. Taxation is actually a good. Without taxation, in the modern world there would be no universal education, no public health service, no public sanitation, no street lighting and so many other things we tend to take for granted, all enabled through taxation. (This view is usually disputed by the anarchists and extreme libertarians; the latter believing that all these facilities may be largely provided through the free 'marketplace'.) So although the book is based on the premise that taxation in general is a good, there are undoubtedly good and bad taxes, or at least taxes that vary in the degree of benefit or harm they might do in their manner of application. In this respect I try to show why LVT is a beneficial tax. I attempt to explain how we might reduce or even eliminate the seemingly endless problem of poverty, which still exists in this 'enlightened' age, through an intelligent and fair system of taxation based on the use of the land we all need.

Although the suggestion of taxing land values may come as a novelty to many, it is actually an old idea, which can be traced back at least to the 18th century economic philosopher Adam Smith. In his book *The Wealth of Nations*, published in 1776, he advocated the taxing of ground rents.[1]

However most contemporary theories on land value taxation are derived largely from the work of the American political economist Henry George and his book *Progress and Poverty*, published in 1879, which is still the definitive source.[2]

Adam Smith proposed four maxims of taxation, which still provide the starting point for all discussions on taxation today. In simplified terms they are, Proportionality (ability to pay), Certainty, Convenience (for the taxpayer) and Efficiency, all of which, I suggest, are well accounted for by LVT.[3] In the first maxim, Proportionality, he states: 'The subjects of every state ought to contribute towards the support of government...' His use of the word 'contribute' is worth noting. The same word is employed by the economist and philosopher William Petty, in an earlier work, published in 1662, which he entitled: *A Treatise of Taxes and Contributions*. Also, the Oxford Dictionary defines 'Tax' as 'a contribution to state revenue compulsorily levied on individuals, property or businesses.'

The use of the word 'contribution' is interesting in that it probably best describes the real nature and basis of taxation. In the above examples taxes are seen more in the form of contributions, and I believe this distinction would help us better understand the constant dilemma that faces all modern governments. Contributions are generally understood to be voluntary whereas taxes are imposed. If we were able to see the payment of taxes more as contributions towards the proper functioning of society within which we operate, with all its amenities and advantages, the unfortunately negative view of taxation might be modified for the better. It is interesting to note that the payments we currently make towards our health and pension provisions are labelled as contributions rather than a tax.

In a properly functioning fair and just society, which still remains an ideal for many (not least the anarchists and libertarians), it is possible to envisage the payment of taxes being seen not as a burden but as a privilege. This happy state may be some time in the future but it is still something worth striving for, and the proposal here is that a land value tax would help towards that end.

The main claim is that LVT is a fair tax, and this is one of the most important of all the arguments that I put forward. In most investigations and reports into people's attitudes towards taxation, the one issue that emerges time and again is the one of fairness. People are always acutely aware of whether some piece of legislation is fair, especially with regard to taxes. The legislators generally claim to have fairness as their first consideration, but so very often the end result in practice falls short of the intention. Those who find a tax onerous and a direct impediment in their lives will see it as unfair, and they are often the majority; the suggestion that they are making their contribution towards society doesn't carry much weight. It's difficult for us to be objective about taxes when they appear to undermine our own best efforts in the constant struggle to improve our personal circumstances.

The American political philosopher Benjamin Franklin was credited with saying 'nothing in this world is certain except death and taxes.'[4]

He was right of course about death but less so about taxes, which being a human invention are not inevitable, or at least are capable of being revised or abolished altogether. It is possible for societies to exist and to prosper without taxes. The early hunter-gatherer tribes had a strong social system, which depended on intense co-operation, but not on taxes; it may have been primitive by our standards, but it worked for them; it was their form of 'economy'. In later, perhaps more barbaric times, warrior societies would thrive on the results of conquest and plunder; taxes didn't come into it. In his book, *Moneyland*, Oliver Bullough quotes the American sociologist Mancur Olson as saying that the origin of civilisation could be traced back to the moment when:

> Roving bandits realised that instead of raiding groups of humans and moving on, they could earn more by staying put and stealing from their victims all the time.[5]

The ancient Romans on the other hand pursued a sensible policy of pacification. Once a territory had been conquered, they did not continue with destruction and pillage but attempted to assimilate the conquered tribes into a colonial system, whereby they could thereafter collect tribute from the general wealth that inevitably arose from peaceful production. As the local people became more Romanised, this naturally evolved into a system of taxation organised by authorised tax collectors, the Publicani, who certainly enriched themselves and often abused the system. But the Publicani were also charged with supervising public works such as roads and bridges, so there was some degree of benefit to the general populace.

Where the wealthy were concerned, the Roman tax collectors identified and measured their wealth by the size of estates, head of cattle the number of slaves etc., for the less wealthy, by a simple poll tax which, however brutal, was a very effective way of resolving the twin problems of identification and measurement: anyone with a head was identifiable and counting the numbers gave the measure. These two factors have always been of concern to the tax collector; how to identify wealth and how to measure it for the purpose of raising revenue, and they continue to be of concern to the present day. The main thing about tax that has usually concerned the taxpayer is how to avoid paying it. Tax avoidance has always been present throughout the whole history of taxation.

The English tax collectors of the 17th century were equally concerned with how to identify the existence of wealth and how to measure it. In an attempt to resolve this permanent problem, in 1662, parliament introduced the method of taxing hearths, the number of which, for each household, was seen as an indication of wealth: the obvious external identification was evident in the number of chimneys. But the tax collectors still required entry into each dwelling to check on each room, an intrusion that was bitterly resented. However bizarre it might seem to us now, there was nevertheless an attempt at fairness.

Similar to the present-day council tax there were seven bands of imposition related to the number of hearths; the lowest band was for the very poor (who could apply for an exemption), and the highest band, seven or over, for the wealthiest. So, however rough and ready, there was some recognition of the idea of progressive taxation. Of course, people engaged in avoidance by blocking off chimneys, but if this was discovered by the tax collector the tax was doubled as a penalty.[6] The hearth tax was highly unpopular and abolished in 1689.

The infamous window tax lasted somewhat longer (1696–1851) and was yet another attempt to identify and measure wealth. The more windows you owned, the wealthier you were, and these, of course, were readily visible without the need of entry. As the window tax lasted over 150 years it was arguably more successful than the hearth tax, but it was also highly unpopular and, as is well known, people resorted to avoidance by bricking up windows.

Tax avoidance has now become a legitimate industry, which thrives on the complexities of income tax, VAT and corporation tax, enabling clever accountants to devise ingenious avoidance schemes, aided by tax lawyers who keep them from straying into the illegality of evasion. The interesting point in all this is that from ancient times to the present day the tax collectors have always had the same three problems, how to identify wealth, how to establish a measure for taxing it and how to deal with avoidance. As I hope will be explained in these pages, a tax based on land values addresses all of these issues in a way that is fair and comprehensible to everyone.

Land values, or on a smaller scale site values, are an indicator of the relative prosperity of different areas within a town, a city or a country, and are therefore an indicator of relative wealth or the capacity to create wealth which, in the urban context, varies according to location. Land values are not a matter of luck, they are the consequence of generations of economic activity of the whole of society and the measure of the demand of that society to work or reside, for whatever reason, in certain areas rather than others. The value in question is created by the whole community and not by any particular activity of the person owning or occupying the land or site. The benefits of the value thus created by the community belong to that community, and this is the main justification for a land value tax.

Politicians devote a lot of time telling voters how they are going to spend their money; they avoid the rather more difficult problem of where to get the money from. LVT is about the latter. Any fool can spend money; it requires a rather higher degree of ability in knowing how to raise it. On listening to reports of current problems with public services: the schools, the police, the prisons, the NHS, the social services, in almost every case the basic cause of the problem can be boiled down to funding. This is disgraceful in a wealthy advanced economy such as Britain's. We British seem to take a curious pride in being able to do everything 'on a shoestring', perhaps a relic of the enforced austerities of World War Two. But things are not getting done anymore and this attitude is no longer good enough. Many people, who are not necessarily poor, but nevertheless dependent on the proper functioning of public services, are not being well served by the current parsimony of the government and the grossly complex and wasteful taxation systems that we have devised over many years.

In a report for the Labour Party published in June 2019, entitled *Land for the Many,* the authors note that land now accounts for 51% of the UK's net worth, and has increased in value from £1 trillion in 1995 to over £5 trillion in 2019.[7] A 1% tax on £5 trillion would render the exchequer £50 billion a year in revenue. This would provide the government with an enormous revenue source and go a long way in helping to resolve the many problems of funding. Even allowing that, under a tax neutrality principle, much of the extra revenue would be used in reducing other deleterious taxes such as income tax, corporation tax and VAT.

So, you might well ask if this wonderful new source of revenue is there for the taking, why has it not been exploited before? Well, the answer is that it has, and has been for many years, for many centuries even, by landowners and land speculators—and this leads inevitably to the issue of the 'rentier' system under which we still live, where land is concerned. The rentier is someone who derives an income by charging a rental for the land simply due to ownership, without making any reciprocal contribution. This rental is known as the 'economic rent', as it is paid from the economic activity on the land carried out by the tenant.

Traditionally, the rentier class were that group of absentee landowners who received an income from their land but lived elsewhere and did not necessarily even take an interest in how the income arose. The play is the same today, but the cast of characters is different; in his book *The State We're In*, Will Hutton comments, 'Pension funds and insurance companies have become the classic absentee landlords, exerting power without responsibility...'[8]

The phrase 'without making any reciprocal contribution' is crucial here, for it distinguishes the parasitic rentier from the genuine owner who, for example, rents out his house, or the investor/shareholder who lends his money for the income from interest, albeit unearned. The ownership of any man-made object or institution, or of knowledge or skill, has always been accepted as legitimate and therefore saleable or rentable. Unfortunately, the ownership of land, made by nature, is also commonly seen as not only legitimate but necessary; but this idea is challenged in this book.

Whereas the rentier may be seen as a passive exploiter, the land speculator is not only active but pro-active. His pernicious mode of operation is explained in the diagrammatic texts of Chapter 2. The claim in this book is that the operations of both the rentier and the land speculator would be curtailed if not eliminated by the introduction of LVT, and so the greatest opposition would therefore arise from those with vested interests in these activities.

I would briefly summarise the main points of the chapters as follows:

Chapter 1 is about basic principles and the main characteristics of LVT.

Chapter 2 makes use of diagrams, which take the reader step by step through the evolution of a society from simple beginnings to the development of a complex city, how land values arise in this process, and why they become a proper basis for a system of taxation. The diagrams also show the distinction between rural and urban land values and how the latter are determined by location within an agglomeration.

Chapters 3 to 6 deal with various aspects of LVT as listed in the Contents.

Chapter 7 deals entirely with the issue of housing, which at the present time is of great concern to the whole populace, but also to the politicians, who appear incapable of improving the situation—whatever clever schemes they introduce. LVT could help to resolve the housing crisis, where a great many not-rich/not-poor homeowners, who have benefitted enormously from the increase in house prices, ironically have to act as bankers for their own children who cannot afford to buy a home.

Chapter 8 describes how under the present system, the economic rent may be collected by private owners in advance, or more deviously by absorption.

Chapter 9 deals with typical objections, which are raised time and again by those opposed to LVT. It also deals with what I see as the main obstacles to be overcome.

Chapter 10 discusses the Single Tax issue and also which other taxes might be reduced, eliminated or kept.

Chapter 11 discusses welfare and how it is inextricably bound up with taxation in Britain as a welfare state.

Chapter 12 is simply a summary of the main points that have been made in the book.

Chapter 13 is about definitions and might well be read first so that any misunderstanding of terms could be avoided.

At the end of the book I have added three appendices: The first is a brief explanation of the prevailing neoclassical economic system, which is difficult to reconcile with the principles that underlie LVT. The second and third items are case studies related to situations in the past where LVT has been adopted over long periods, but eventually abandoned.

Opponents would say that the reasons were because LVT failed. However, I believe the cases show that LVT was abandoned because it was successful—but not in the interests of powerful landowners and fearful time serving politicians. In the introduction to his book *Land Value Taxation Around the World*, Robert Andelson states:

> The system has in some few cases been abolished, but never because it was a failure.[9]

Readers will no doubt make their own judgement.

During my studies of economics, I recollect it being said that the first law of economics is that 'the strong owe a duty towards the weak.' This comment always stuck in my mind, and if it were to be fully observed,

I believe so many of our economic problems and difficulties would be resolved, indeed they would not arise in the first place. This ethical aspect of economics is nothing new; throughout the ages writers on political philosophy have always expressed concern on the issues of justice and the plight of the poor. It goes back to ancient times. In his book *The Possibility of Progress,* Mark Braund refers to the ancient Babylonian law code of Hammurabi, which required that 'the strong might not oppress the weak.'[10]

Thankfully, this element of compassion has always been observed within the family; parents care for their children, who in turn care for their parents in their old age, although there are unfortunately more and more occasions where these obvious duties are neglected. However, even in this hard materialistic world there are many instances of charitable giving and philanthropy. People generally want to be kind and generous, but it is difficult for them to be so if they are themselves suffering from economic deprivation, a deprivation that arises mainly from a disregard of this first law. The law is clearly about duties rather than rights.

But there are reasons for optimism. There are a growing number of individuals and organisations, which are aware of the abuses and injustices of the present economic settlement and are working towards reform—and they are being taken notice of. Not least of these is a group of wealthy people who describe themselves as Patriotic Millionaires, who believe they should pay more tax; an encouraging sign that rich people themselves are aware of the increasing wealth gap, and that the current tax system is unfair. They explain their position in a book, *Tax the Rich,* co-authored by Morris Pearl and Erica Payne.[11] The group originated in the US in 2010. In October 2021 thirty members of the UK branch petitioned the chancellor to tax them more highly.[12]

It has to be acknowledged that any move towards a system of land value taxation would represent a massive change in the whole concept of taxation and our attitudes towards the ownership of property. It would mean unravelling centuries of malpractice and would therefore have to be introduced carefully and gradually. It would need to gain the support of taxpayers, being convinced that it was a fair and equitable system. It would also be dependent for its success on a comprehensive system of regular valuations, established at the outset, rigorously maintained and open to public scrutiny.

You might well wonder whether LVT has any limitations. Well, yes it does. It is not a panacea to solve all taxation problems. As its name implies it is a matter associated only with society's relationship to land, which is absolutely fundamental but not the only issue in the complex world of economics. There are similar issues to be resolved: the ongoing scandals of tax havens, lobbying, money laundering, and the creation of money itself, all of which have an impact on the everyday lives of honest hard-working citizens. But as with the issue of land, they are constantly deferred by the complacent forces of an establishment untouched by the iniquities of the system, or even benefitting from it.

Many eminent economists, scholars and literary figures have expressed their support for LVT since the time Henry George published his book *Progress and*

Poverty, but perhaps the admiration for George's ideas was best expressed in a letter written by Albert Einstein to George's daughter in 1934, in which he said:

> Men like Henry George are rare unfortunately. One cannot imagine a more beautiful combination of intellectual keenness, artistic form and fervent love of justice. Every line is written as if for our generation.[13]

After several generations since this was written perhaps it is time we took some action.

The material for this book is derived mainly from my website, Land Value Tax Guide: http://landvaluetaxguide.com, which can be referred to where you might find it more convenient to follow up links on-line.

.

CHAPTER 1

BASIC PRINCIPLES

The economic case for a land value tax is simple and almost undeniable. Why then do we not have one already? Why hasn't it been adopted widely in the western world? Even more puzzling is that, right now, as western economies struggle with the global financial crisis, why isn't this form of taxation being seriously considered as an alternative?

Sir James Mirrlees (1936–2018): Nobel economics laureate and chairman of the Mirrlees Review, *Tax by Design,* published in 2011

I suggest there are four basic principles or characteristics of LVT that may be expressed under the headings:

1. Community created value.
2. Taxation according to means.
3. A direct tax.
4. Simplicity and clarity.

1.1 Community Created Value

This is the principle of returning to the community, by means of a tax or levy, the value that the community itself has created. This value is measured through land values, which are simply an indication of collective prosperity. With the growth of a community, the value of any site will increase due to the surrounding communal activity or community-funded infrastructure that has the effect of enhancing the value of the site. This increased value falls fortuitously to the benefit of the owner and may be realised in the form of increased rents or capital value at any point of sale. The revenue thus derived is not due to any work done by the owner and is clearly unearned. It is known by economists as the 'economic rent of land' (generally abbreviated to the 'economic rent').

The classical economists, from Adam Smith onwards, were aware of this source of revenue, however it was David Ricardo in his *Principles of Political Economy and Taxation*, of 1817, who first identified the economic rent (see Chapter 13, Definitions). The economic rent still exists, it has never gone away, it is still collected and it still goes into private pockets. The prime purpose of LVT is not to stop this collection but to re-channel it into the public coffers, thereby returning to the community the value that it has created.

The difference between the terms 'land value' and 'site value' as used here, is simply a matter of scale. Land value is the term used when applied to a large geographical area, within which there are many sites. It is more often used in the rural situation. Land value is therefore an expression of the aggregate of all the site values within the area under consideration. The term site value is more appropriately used in the urban context, where the areas concerned are smaller. One may have specific high value sites within an area of general low prosperity and low value sites within an area of general high prosperity.

The value of any property has two parts: the value of the building—the bricks and mortar—and the value of the site. Unlike the building value, the site value, in the urban situation, is determined by its location within the community. As most estate agents would concur, where property valuations are concerned, it is more a question of 'where' rather than 'what'— primarily a matter of location. In the urban context, it would not be incorrect to describe LVT as a location value tax, where the value of a particular site is determined by communal demand at that particular location.

It should also be noted that LVT is proposed as a replacement tax, not an additional tax. To the degree that it is introduced, other taxes should be proportionately reduced or eliminated; the overall tax take would remain the same.

1.2 Taxation According to Means

Taxation according to means is an essential characteristic of any fair tax system. Where this happens, the tax is described as 'progressive.' With LVT the tax burden is imposed according to relative prosperity as measured by land values. The word relative is important here for the practicability of LVT depends on land value differentials. The theory is that these differentials distinguish between areas of high and low prosperity, which are then taxed accordingly. If all land had the same uniform value, there would be no basis for a land value tax. In such a situation a land value tax would be little better than a poll tax, where the measure is on the number of acres rather than the number of heads.

There is always an ongoing discussion amongst politicians and their advisors about where and how taxes should be imposed. The possibilities seem limitless: incomes, sales, transactions, capital gains, property, road use and so on. Rarely is there much agreement; the left say, 'tax the rich', the right say tax anything except the rich, who they claim are the 'wealth creators.' Nevertheless, whatever the type of tax, there are, I suggest, two basic principles that apply to all taxes:

1. That every able-bodied, able-minded adult who benefits from belonging to a society should make a contribution towards its upkeep.
2. Such contribution should be in accordance with the ability to pay.

Most people would agree with these principles as being fair and reasonable. The first is probably beyond dispute—one could reasonably argue that simply being a member of a community is a benefit in itself. It is with the second that disagreement usually arises, basically over the interpretation of the expression 'ability to pay'. Most would agree with the old Marxist dictum 'From each according to his abilities, to each according to his needs', but much disagreement arises with the definitions of 'abilities' and 'needs'. However, no one has expressed it better, and it remains a guiding principle for all systems of fair taxation.

Taxation of any kind has always involved identification and measurement: identifying what might be taxed and ascertaining to what degree the tax might be imposed, taking into account the means of the payer; that is his ability to pay. This latter consideration has given rise to the principle of progressive taxation, where those most able to bear a tax should pay more in proportion to their wealth or apparent prosperity. Land values provide a measurement of such prosperity whereby the occupiers or owners of high-value sites are generally considered more prosperous, and therefore better able to bear a tax, than those on low-value sites. This may be seen as a blunt instrument of measurement, but it is nevertheless generally true.

1.3 A Direct Tax

LVT has the advantage of being a direct tax. One of the arguments against indirect taxes is that they are indiscriminate—they are paid equally by the rich and poor alike and are therefore unfair. However, they are popular with governments, as they allow the people to believe that they are not really being taxed, they are simply paying higher prices. This phenomenon was noted by Adam Smith, who, in discussing taxes on commodities, commented that 'the consumer, who finally pays them, soon comes to confound them with the price of the commodities, and almost forgets that he pays any tax.'[1]

Indirect taxes also seem to be preferred by taxpayers, for the reason that they are impersonal and clearly paid by everyone equally, no doubt appealing to a sense of fairness, regardless of the fact that the poor pay the same as the rich. Also, indirect taxes are convenient for governments as they are more flexible, being easily adjustable to meet unexpected events without constant reference to electoral promises, and so they are undeniably useful, but for the reasons mentioned above it is better if they are kept to a minimum. Direct taxes, I suggest, are more honest, and I believe, in the long run it is better for governments to be honest with the people.

Direct taxes may be divided into two basic groups:

1. Taxes imposed on existing wealth.
2. Taxes imposed on the wealth-creation process.

To encourage wealth creation and general prosperity it is always better to levy taxes on the first group rather than the second. The first are taxes on ownership, the second are taxes on work and trade.

Among the first group are property taxes (Council Tax and Business Rates), Capital Gains Tax and Inheritance Tax. Capital Gains Tax is more accurately a tax on the realisation of increased value at the point of a sale. Inheritance Tax is a tax on the realisation of value at the time of a transfer of wealth, but they are both taxes on existing wealth. None of these taxes are impediments to wealth creation.

Among the second group are Earned Income Tax* and Employee's National Insurance Contributions, which are taxes on work. Also, included are VAT, Corporation Tax and Stamp Duty, which are taxes on

---

* Unearned income (on interest, for example) should be taxed under existing wealth.

trade. These taxes act as discouragements to wealth creation. LVT would fall into the first group as a tax on unearned wealth, actual or potential, due to the simple ownership of land—one of the essential elements of production. This would include vacant land being held out of use for speculative purposes. Although land is not in itself wealth (see Chapter 13, Definitions) it is one of the two elements that are necessary for (physical) wealth creation, the other being labour. The ownership of either element implies the ownership of the means to wealth creation.

1.4 Simplicity and Clarity

An important characteristic of LVT, which many other taxes do not enjoy, is its openness, clarity and predictability, which makes it a tax that would be difficult to avoid. With LVT, the basis of the tax would be obvious and apparent to all. Site values would be regularly assessed and published for public scrutiny. The tax due on any site could be calculated by anyone. The figures could not be hidden behind 'creative accounting' or aggressive tax avoidance schemes. Furthermore, land cannot be moved offshore to a convenient tax haven. A tax-avoidance industry, which costs the exchequer billions in lost revenue each year, would be impossible with LVT. Income Tax, VAT and Corporation Tax provide a happy hunting ground for sharp practitioners who flourish in the complexity and obscurity that such taxes allow.

Under LVT, private ownership of land could continue although land speculation as such would disappear.

Excessive increases of house prices, which are caused through the increase of the land-value factor, would be brought under control. Sites would continue to be bought and sold, but any prospective purchaser would know in advance the tax obligation for any site and would be able to enter such commitment into his calculations. There would need to be regular and comprehensive valuations, which would be accessible to all as a matter of public information at all times, as are the existing public registers for Council Tax and Business Rates.

CHAPTER 2

ECONOMIC EVOLUTION

No tribe has the right to sell, even to each other,
much less to strangers. Sell a country! Why not
sell the air, the great sea, as well as the earth?
Didn't the Great Spirit make them all for the use
of his children?

Tecumseh (1768–1813), Chief of the Shawnee tribe

A Diagrammatic Explanation

A good way of explaining LVT is through a series of
diagrams showing how land values arise from the first
settlement of virgin territory through its evolution to a
large community, and the best example of this is the
settlement and development of North America.
The column diagrams that follow show the economic
growth of a community from very simple beginnings,
where each column represents the productivity on
each site. All real wealth derives from work, physical
or mental, and in the earliest settlements this was
almost exclusively due to agrarian work applied directly
to the land.

Figure 1 represents the productivity of the first site
settled and worked by one man and his family. The

settler has an abundance of choice from equally fertile sites and the column represents the maximum production he can achieve to support himself and his family on the site he selects.

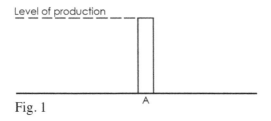

Fig. 1

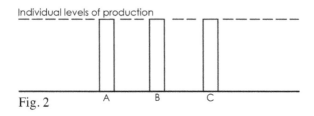

Fig. 2

Figure 2 shows two further sites settled and worked with similar results, giving a general level of productivity by settlers working independently on sites of similar fertility, assuming equality of work done by each settler. In reality although the sites may well be physically adjacent, as they are worked independently, they are shown as separate in the diagram.

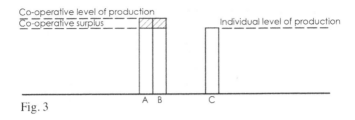

Fig. 3

In Figure 3 two of the settlers decide that it is mutually beneficial to work in co-operation to effect what neither would be able to do alone. Their total combined product is therefore more than twice the product of each working separately. This additional product may be described as a co-operative surplus. The decision of A and B to co-operate is the first step in the creation of an economy. Economics begins with and depends on interaction. This principle is fundamental to any understanding of LVT—the idea of co-operation is paramount. Economics as such begins at this point, when men co-operate to act collectively. When the three settlers were operating independently an economic community had not come into being. When A and B agreed to co-operate an economic relationship was established.

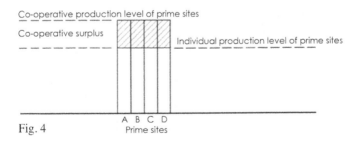

Fig. 4

In Figure 4 settlers C and D have joined the embryonic community and the overall product increases accordingly. It is reasonable to assume that the settlers will choose what they see as the best sites, which may be described as 'prime sites.' At this stage it can be seen that the production on each site is equal, and the original production level, common to all sites, becomes a useful reference datum to maintain through the subsequent diagrams.

Each new settler is naturally attracted to join the existing community and with each addition the co-operative surplus increases with greater efficiency through more specialisation (generally described by economists as 'the division of labour'). In this simple community the distribution of the surplus product would be shared equally for equal work done, as yet there are no taxes. Neither is there any need for money, for after all how could it be spent? Whatever transactions take place, are in kind, or the exchange of labour. The level of this co-operative production rises with each new member of the community but is still the same for all sites, which are of equal productivity. At this stage the growing community is still characterised by equality: of work done, production achieved, distribution of benefits and values of the respective sites.

When the prime sites are all taken, the next settler will have to take a site that is less productive (in agrarian terms), a so-called marginal site (site E, Figure 5). However, his production will still be superior to that which he could achieve independently. He will receive the benefit from the co-operative surplus as well as contributing towards it. His independent production level is shown (theoretically) as lower than that of the production of the original prime sites. Marginal sites will be occupied and worked as long as they provide the occupant with a viable living and where the product is more than could be achieved working independently.

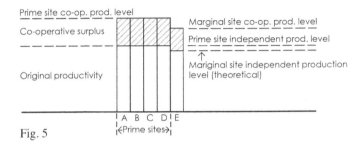

Fig. 5

The level of production at the margin will, in later development, become an important factor in the economic arrangement. The appearance of the margin has created the first manifestation of a differential in land values, albeit due to the reduced value of site E. However, this difference is largely caused by the physical condition of site E within an agrarian economy, due for instance to reduced fertility or the lack of a natural water source. It is site E itself that is different, nothing has changed on the prime sites. The apparent advantage of the prime sites is due to the disadvantage of site E. The theoretical marginal-site independent production level is shown in the diagram for the sake of comparison.

Figure 6 shows the next phenomenon—positive advantage due to location.

At the same time as more marginal sites are occupied, adding to the co-operative surplus, a positive difference

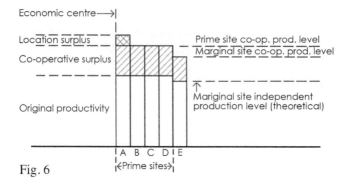

Fig. 6

in productive advantage arises on certain sites due entirely to their location in relation to all the others. Though no increase of work on the sites has taken place they will become more productively advantageous due to their proximity to the centre of economic activity. They may not necessarily be at the geographic centre of the community, but rather at the economic centre, perhaps where the community chooses to hold a market, or where a crossroads arises.

In Figure 6, site A shows this additional productivity, which may be termed a location surplus, and it is this surplus that provides the principal justification for a land value tax. This location surplus introduces a second differential in land values, which has a different cause to the first. The first is due to decreased fertility, an act of nature, the second is a man-made phenomenon, due to the existence and growth of a community. It is this second type of differential that will be the future basis for LVT. Certainly, the manifestation of location value would appear on the prime sites first as they would already be at the centre of the community. This would be due to their positive advantage of location and have little to do with any advantage of fertility.

The community as it grows will, for whatever reason, naturally form an economic centre of gravity, and those that benefit from this will do so by the simple good fortune of their location. It is this fact of location that will outweigh all others as an advantage as a community grows to eventually become a large city. The important point to acknowledge is that this increase of value is not due to any particular activity on the site itself, but to the collective activity of all the sites as an economic whole. One may say that this collective activity gives rise to a centripetal economic pressure. This pressure causes certain sites to become more valuable within a community the nearer they are to the economic centre.

The foregoing is a description in principle of how differential land values arise. This same principle holds good throughout the subsequent development of the small community into a great thriving metropolis with very high land values. Nothing in this process changes the principle that these differential values are created by the whole community, and, for that reason, may be considered a proper source for taxation.

With continuing growth, the community transforms from a mainly agrarian to a more commercial urban base, and the more valuable sites are at the centres of commerce and trade. In our simple early community, a general store might be established on what is seen as the most advantageous location, followed by a hotel and other amenities, so consolidating the establishment of an economic centre. Each new arrival adds to the overall prosperity increasing the pressure on the more valuable sites and thereby increasing the location surplus (see Figure 7).

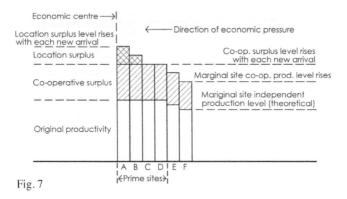

Fig. 7

It must be remembered that these diagrams are useful only to explain the principles involved. In reality, a community is a living dynamic organism, which evolves on all fronts at the same time. As will be shown later, the datum provided by the original agrarian prime site level will eventually be replaced by the datum of the marginal level, from which the location surplus will thereafter be measured.

Up to this point the diagrams have been based on the growth of a fundamentally agrarian society. However, the more a society grows the more it transforms its basic activities to commerce and trade. The measure of productivity, and therefore the value of a site, will move away from considerations of fertility and proximity to the market to more commercially based criteria. The economic centre will move to where the action is; for example, the construction of a bridge may provide a new centre for trade. Sites previously considered marginal may well become more valuable because of their location, and this is the nub of the matter: location is all-important. The previous significance of agrarian prime site production diminishes as society moves to commerce and trade. However, the basic causes of the co-operative surplus and the location surplus do not change.

As the community grows, productivity increases on all sites, but the increase is now due to commercial rather than agrarian activity. In this transformation to urban development, the prime sites A, B, C and D, will be favoured; production now being more a question of profitability for the occupier in whatever form that can be achieved.

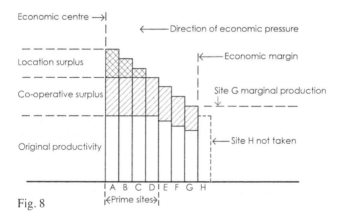

Fig. 8

Figure 8 shows an even gradation of differential values from the highest production on site A to the newest marginal site G. Where marginal sites are freely available, the prospective occupier will be free to decide for himself whether to exploit the site on his own account or work for another for wages. (The subject of wages will be discussed later, together with employment and the issue of speculation).

As the community develops the productivity due to agricultural activity remains relatively static, whereas that due to commercial activity increases on all sites.

In Figure 9, when site H is finally taken it will be because the productivity is more than the occupant can achieve outside the community. It is still worthwhile for any newcomer to join the prospering community and to benefit from the co-operative surplus. Figure 9 shows continuing growth where sites A, B, C and D are all showing locational advantage, for commercial reasons, whereas their original agrarian production level remains the same. The agrarian based levels of production have by now become completely overtaken by the commercial levels, and the new margin is at a higher level than the original productivity of the prime sites.

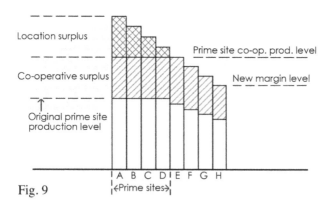

Fig. 9

So far in the diagrams the agrarian levels of production have been useful in explaining how the co-operative surplus arises as an integral part of the economic process but in the new commercial situation the agrarian criteria become increasingly redundant and are shown in Figure 9 purely for theoretical comparison. For clarity they will be omitted from Figure 10 onwards, where only the commercial margin level will be used as the new datum. Henceforth the diagrams are based on urban rather than agrarian values. This new urban datum line now becomes the level from which to measure values due to location.

From this point onwards it is the level of production at the margin that will provide the reference base for further economic development, in particular relating to the issues of wages, employment and speculation. However, it has to be remembered that all production below the level due to location always comprises an element due to co-operation. All communities depend on co-operation and interaction if they are to prosper. Although it may not be readily apparent it is always there; it is the glue that holds a community together and provides the future foundation for location values.[1] Interaction also includes competition as well as co-operation. This is shown where certain activities and trades group together for mutual benefit but still remain in competition.

Wages and Employment

From the very earliest stages of development, on the more productive sites, an occupant may decide that it is more profitable to employ labour to carry out the work. To attract the labour the wages offered will need to be higher than an individual can achieve working independently on a marginal site. This level of wages will therefore be related to the alternative level of earnings at the margin. The level of wages offered will depend on the supply and demand of labour. Where labour is scarce the level will rise above the marginal site level; where it is abundant it will tend to fall below, and new marginal sites will be occupied in preference. In general, where land is freely available these levels will tend to track each other (see Figure 10).

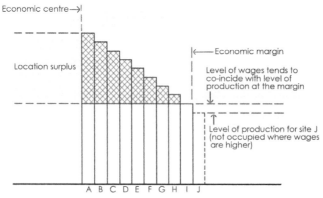

Fig.10   Wages, where land is freely available

Where land is not freely available (due to enclosure or prior claims to ownership) the prospective settlers will be forced to seek their fortune elsewhere or work for wages at a depressed level.

Tenancy

In the early years of settlement in North America the settlers were simply squatters on land previously used freely by the Native Americans who had no concept of land ownership. The settlers staked out as much land as they could use and proceeded to work it. Over time, due to their responsible occupation, their appropriation went unchallenged and became quasi-ownership through custom and usage. Their claim to ownership was, no doubt helped by the ideas of the political philosopher John Locke—that work carried out on the land was a justification for ownership (see Chapter 5, Ownership of Land). Their efforts towards ownership were also helped by pre-emption laws that allowed them to buy small areas of land at minimum prices.[2]

On the more productive sites owner/occupiers could choose to employ labour directly or rent all or part of their land to a tenant, who paid a rent out of his earnings from the land he worked. The rental value to the owner was thus related to the productive value of the site. It is this annual rental value of land that is later to become the preferred basis for calculating the rate of LVT.

Land Speculation

The US Federal government was always interested in encouraging the settlement and development of territory westward. To this end, in 1785, it introduced an ordinance in which lots of 640 acres of land could be sold off at $2 an acre.[3] Unfortunately this opportunity was exploited by land speculators who had no intention of working the land themselves. They bought up large areas, which they then held out of use, waiting for values to rise so they could make a good profit from renting or selling later at a higher price. This of course prevented new settlers from gaining access to viable sites. An even lower margin was thus created beyond the enclosed land held out of use, which further depressed the level of wages (see Figure 11).

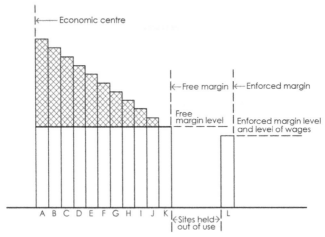

Fig.11   Wages, depressed by land speculation

The speculators were able to make great fortunes selling off individual sites at high profits as the land values rose with increasing demand. This type of speculation continues to this day and is especially damaging in newly developing countries.

In a fully developed community, the site values would range from the minimum at the margin to the maximum at the economic centre. In reality the differences in values are always steeper towards the economic centre and more gradual towards the margin. Figure 12 has been drawn to show this distinction, where the closer one approaches the centre the greater are the differences, whereas sites towards the margin, which are more

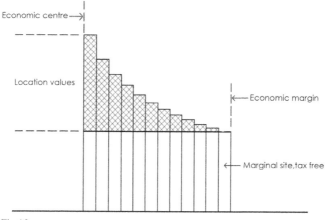

Fig.12

numerous, will have differences that progressively diminish.

All communities will develop an economic centre, which will arise naturally with any economic activity, not necessarily near any geographic centre, but nevertheless fairly well defined within a limited area. On the other hand, the economic margin will be less well defined, being determined simply by the decision of any potential occupier as to whether the return achievable on any site is worthwhile, compared to the alternative of working for wages, or trying another community altogether.

In later development, a large city may have numerous local centres as well as a principal centre with the highest site values. Low value sites may occur anywhere between these centres but the true margin of activity will be at the periphery of the whole agglomeration. Within a developing community the economic centre will not be fixed either in character or position. An earlier centre may well be overtaken by another centre related to other activities, but one thing they will all have in common is that the communal demand to occupy the sites will determine their value.

It is worth noting that within a typical concentric form of growth, valuable sites at the centre are few, whereas sites at the margin are numerous. Also, as was shown earlier, the least productive sites at the margin contribute to the value of the sites at the centre. As LVT is to be taken only from above the level of the margin it is clear that the marginal site, by definition, would always be tax free.

CHAPTER 3

APPLICATION AND ADVANTAGES

As soon as the land of any country has all become private property, the landlords, like all other men, love to reap where they never sowed, and demand a rent even for its natural produce.

Adam Smith, *The Wealth of Nations,* 1776

3.1 Application of LVT

LVT may be described as a levy that society imposes for the exclusive occupation and use of a site. The use to which the site is put may or may not be for wealth-creation purposes. For instance, where a site is occupied for a purely residential purpose, the levy is still payable according to the value of the site. Also, the owner of an unused or derelict site would still pay the tax, for the site would retain its potential value whether used or not. This would discourage the deliberate holding of sites out of use for speculative purposes. As with most property taxes, there would need to be an appeals system. With LVT, valuations could always be challenged, but these would be more likely on the high value sites rather than near the margin, where the tax burden would be less.

LVT should be introduced gradually without any sudden shock, over a transition period of ten years or more during which other unsuitable taxes—for example, those that are impediments to wealth creation—could be reduced or eliminated. As LVT is proposed as a replacement tax, not an additional tax, the overall receipts from all taxes would remain the same.

All taxes have an economic or social effect. Taxes on a commodity will affect the production and purchase of the commodity—for instance taxes on trade will inhibit trading. Certain taxes are designed deliberately to affect social behaviour rather than to simply raise revenue, for example eco-taxes and the so-called sin taxes.[1] Taxes generally tend to have a negative effect on economic activity—what economists describe as a 'deadweight loss'—where the imposition of the tax may negatively affect its efficiency in raising revenue, even to the point where the burden is so great that economic activity ceases.

Most taxes suffer from this defect: income tax is a discouragement to work, VAT is a discouragement to trade, and so on. LVT would have no deadweight loss because land supply is fixed and the imposition of the tax will neither increase nor decrease supply. Neither will any increase nor decrease of economic activity on the site affect its value for the value is determined by other external factors (see Chapter 5: Causes of Land Value). With accurate and regular valuations, the tax would be easy to collect; there would be little wastage and no avoidance. For these reasons LVT may be seen as an efficient tax, and most economists agree on this point at least.

A tax on land values would bring about a reduction of values by bringing land held out of use for speculative purposes onto the market, but it would not otherwise increase the overall amount. Though the value might alter, it would, through a comprehensive valuation system, be visible to everyone, and could not be obscured. LVT would cause a shift in the burden of overall taxation away from the margin towards the centre; away from less prosperous areas onto the more prosperous, as measured by location values. Thus, it would satisfy the requirement that taxes should be paid in accordance with the ability to pay.

In an established system of LVT one might envisage the principal source of revenue coming from LVT, alongside other useful taxes, which are retained (see Chapter 10, Taxes to Eliminate, Modify or Keep). The overall tax take would vary according to government requirements, which, in the case of LVT, could be reduced due to the efficiency of collection. Where this occurred, any reduction in LVT would be measured 'from the top down', that is to say with a graduated percentage reduction inversely proportional to the site value. This would effectively raise the level of the margin and have the effect of taking more marginal sites out of tax altogether.

A Local or a National Tax?

There are two possibilities for the application of LVT: at a national level or a local level. The introduction of a national LVT would have one major advantage in that it would effect a geographic redistribution of the tax burden nationally, and so reduce the inequalities resulting from the so-called north/south divide (which is more accurately a London-and-the-rest divide). Although a national tax may be preferred in the long term, it would be a very major step, and it is generally felt by LVT advocates that a local system initially would be more feasible where implementation is concerned. Also, there are certain advantages to the introduction at a local level:

- LVT could be trialled in certain selected cities willing to support a pilot scheme.
- As LVT is primarily an urban tax, it would be well suited to local urban councils (as opposed to rural councils).
- LVT could replace Business Rates and Council Tax, which are already functioning with their own valuation systems—however defective.
- There is a better chance of explaining the principles of LVT to taxpayers, who are already paying property taxes.
- Councils could learn from successful applications of local LVT already operating, for example in Harrisburg, Clairton and Allentown in Pennsylvania, US.[2]

Business Rates are an indirect non-domestic tax based on the annual rental value of the property (land and buildings, plus fixed plant or equipment). There is already a working valuation system, updated every five years (last carried out in April 2015). A change made with any system of taxation inevitably causes some to gain and some to lose, but with an indirect tax such as business rates the problem is reduced, or at least de-personalised. For this reason, it would likely be more acceptable to the politicians—businesses do not have the vote. A land-value based business tax would also encourage investments in machinery, equipment and improvements to buildings and physical assets, as these would not be taxed, so there is a lot to be said for replacing business rates with LVT.

The Council Tax by contrast is a direct domestic tax based on the capital value of the property—the market selling price—land and building combined. It is currently based on a valuation system that is virtually defunct, not having been carried out since 1991. This could no doubt be resurrected, given the political will. Replacing the council tax with LVT would accentuate the problem of winners and losers (see Chapter 7, Winners and Losers), but I believe this difficulty has to be faced up to sooner or later; the longer it is left, the worse it will get. The defects of the council tax are explained in more detail in Chapter 7. A regular and reliable valuation system is essential. The neglect of this condition was the main cause that undermined the LVT system in Pittsburgh over the years (see Appendix 3). Another undermining factor is the granting of exemptions and thresholds, usually by politicians hoping to curry favour with the voters: One of the reasons the local land value taxes are so ineffectual in many states in Australia is because of the exemptions and high thresholds on domestic property.

A Transition Period

In all cases a transition period would be essential. Many of the objections raised against LVT are based on the assumption that it would be introduced overnight (as happens quite often when, with a change of government, the new administration abolishes some existing system and introduces its own 'improvements'). Any change to LVT would have to be gradual, measured and designed to cause the least disruption to those affected.

Especially in the case of domestic property a transition period of at least 10 years is suggested.[3] One of the problems with a longer period is in dealing with the impatience of politicians who often believe they have only five years to achieve their purposes, so education is important, not just for politicians but for the voting public in understanding the basic principles of LVT and why it would take time to repair centuries of injustice.

In Andelson's book, *Land Value Taxation Around the World*, Walter Rybeck gives an example of what not to do, with the unfortunate experience of Uniontown, Pennsylvania, which adopted and then rejected LVT in the same year, 1992. The officials introduced the two-rate system abruptly without first correcting the 34-year-old assessments, and without advanced notice. It was of course a disaster. As Rybeck notes, 'Its story is a cautionary tale of how not to introduce a two-rate tax.'[4]

A lesson could also be learnt from the botched introduction of the government's 2010 Universal Credit scheme, which had general cross-party agreement as a good idea in principle, but whose implementation was not properly thought through and has caused much unnecessary hardship, unreasonably bringing the whole idea into disrepute.

A Valuation System

There is no doubt that any successful system of LVT (or any property-based tax) is dependent on an effective valuation system being established and regularly maintained. One of the reasons for the apparent failure of the current council tax is that it is still based on the 1991 valuations, so the tax demands become ever more detached from reality with every year that passes. All politicians and local councillors know this but are unwilling to do anything about it, as they see that a new valuation would create corrections in which there would be losers, so the situation continues to deteriorate.

As well as the example of Uniontown mentioned above, another more long-drawn-out example of the consequences of neglecting the valuation system is described in the case study of Appendix 3: The Pittsburgh Experience. This recounts the split-rate system that operated in Pittsburgh from 1914 to 2001.* For the first 28 years it functioned well, with regular valuations every three years. But after 1942, with a change of administration to a more centralised control, the valuations became irregular and finally neglected, eventually causing the demise of the tax. So it cannot be stressed too much that a regular and reliable valuation process is absolutely essential to any proposed LVT system.

---

* A 'split-rate' is the name employed in the US, where the tax is applied separately in different proportions to the building value and the site value.

3.2 Advantages of LVT

<u>Regional Redistribution</u>

In the UK, at the present time, a considerable amount of taxpayer's money is spent on regional assistance schemes aimed at depressed areas, in order to encourage economic activity and a revival in fortunes for the populace in those areas. A national land value tax would automatically address this problem. It would effect a transfer of the tax burden away from low value areas towards high value areas and so reduce the necessity for such regional aid schemes. The effectiveness of this would of course depend on the condition of tax neutrality—that the introduction of LVT must give rise to an equivalent reduction in other taxes by the same amount. Assuming that the other taxes so reduced are universal—that is, at the same rate throughout the country—then all areas would benefit, poor areas and wealthy areas alike, but only the poor areas would gain the benefit of a lower land value tax, based on location. The wealthier areas would have an equivalent increase, so the wealthier areas would gain and lose while the poorer areas would only gain. In this way there would be a redistribution, not of wealth, but of the surrender of wealth in the form of taxation.

With a national system, the total government receipts would remain the same but they would receive more from the wealthier areas than the poorer areas. This would reduce the need for assistance to the latter, effecting a saving for the national exchequer, which would benefit everyone. Regional assistance is verging on welfare, and may unfortunately be necessary, but people would prefer to help themselves through well-paid work rather than rely on welfare.

Clearly, this benefit of regional redistribution would not arise where LVT was applied only at the local level, for instance where adopted voluntarily by a town or city as an alternative to the council tax. Also, at local level there would be, in most situations, an absence of agricultural land that would be integral to any national tax. At the local level LVT would be primarily an urban tax and therefore, as previously explained, would be well suited to a limited local application. With LVT there would be a redistribution of the tax burden, according to location values, and the tax would provide local authorities an excellent opportunity to regain control over their own finances and their own affairs.

Devolution and Local Taxes

Few governments advocate the most important factor in devolution to the regions; the power to raise revenue. At the present time local government revenues derive from three sources: 52% from council tax, 31% from central government grants and 17% from retained business rates.[5] Prior to 2013 the whole of revenue from business rates was surrendered to central government, which absorbed it into the central grant system for redistribution—at the government's discretion. Since 2013 local councils have been allowed to retain 50% of business rates, and since 2017 various pilot schemes have been trialled with a view to increasing the retention allowance to 100%—which would be preferred by those councils with strong business sectors.

Clearly, local councils are beholden to central government for a large proportion of their funding, which is not a happy place to be. LVT, if applied at the local level, would be an ideal means for giving local authorities real power over their own affairs. If local authorities are not able to raise revenue to finance necessary services they become dependent on support from central government, and as Rolland O'Regan warned in his book, *Rating in New Zealand*: 'Grants and subventions from central government are the kiss of death to local government.'[6] In the ten years from 2010 to 2019, although council taxes in England have been increased by 21%, central government grants have been cut by 38%.[7] So councils are struggling to survive financially and in many cases having to cut services.

Raising revenue for local government has been an intractable problem over the years. The various methods tried—local rates, the community charge and council tax—have all proved unsatisfactory. (For a critique of the council tax refer to Chapter 7, *The Council Tax Deficiency*). A local income tax, as practiced in the US, has also been proposed as a solution. However, in the UK at least, there appears to be a general consensus that any local tax should relate in some way to property and be graduated according to the rentable or capital value of the property. Previous systems have attempted this in different ways, but none has ever directly taken into account one of the most important factors, the value of the site upon which the property stands.

As mentioned in chapter 1, the value of a property has two parts: the value of the building—the bricks and mortar—and the value of the site. A tax on the site value only would resolve many problems. It would remove the current penalty against new building or making improvements. It would encourage the productive use of vacant and 'brownfield'* sites and it would provide a natural system of gradation of relative values.

Restraint of Property Values

The presence of a land value tax would rein in the escalation of property prices and speculation based on constantly increasing location values. Prospective buyers of any property would be aware of the cost of any future land value tax requirement and factor this into their calculations before making an offer. Sellers would have to reduce their asking prices accordingly.

In the housing market, at the present time many wealthy investors buy houses because, as an appreciating asset, they provide a better return than other forms of investment. With LVT this advantage would disappear and investors would move elsewhere. Housing would return to what it should be—a place to live rather than a speculator's means of enrichment.

Although, for these reasons, in the urban context land values would be restrained if not reduced, at the other end of the spectrum—at the margin of agricultural land—values might actually increase. In his book *Location Matters,* Tony Vickers points out:

---

* So-called brownfield sites are usually former industrial sites that remain abandoned or considered too costly to redevelop.

Marginal land would by definition attract no LVT, but the reduction in other taxes would bring land that is currently uneconomic to farm back into profit. Agricultural land values at what is now the margin would rise.[8]

Tax evasion and avoidance

The government relies heavily on income tax to raise revenue, but one of the great weaknesses of income tax is that it is easily subject to evasion by unscrupulous operators. This costs the exchequer countless billions in lost revenue, which of course has to be made good by the honest taxpayer. There is also a thriving legal tax-avoidance industry in which lawyers and accountants devote their time advising us how to be tax-efficient; in other words, how to avoid paying our taxes. All of this depends on the obscurity and ambiguity of the existing tax systems. LVT is a system that would be clear and obvious to all and would eliminate this unproductive activity, which represents an enormous waste of a human resource that could otherwise be employed to some useful purpose.

Taxes, in whatever form, have never been popular. They are usually seen as an unwelcome burden to be borne with resentment and avoided wherever possible. But in an enlightened society the payment of tax would be seen not only as a good but also as a privilege, in being able to contribute to the wellbeing of society. It isn't tax itself that is the problem; it is the type of tax and the means by which it is applied.

CHAPTER 4

HISTORY

Wherever there is great property, there is great inequality. For one very rich man there must be at least five hundred poor.

Adam Smith, *The Wealth of Nations,* 1776

4.1 Early History

LVT has never been introduced in Britain, although the idea has been discussed at both central and local government level, and on several occasions almost been implemented. An early history of the idea of LVT may be traced and summarised chronologically through the following events and publications:

1662. Publication of *The Treatise of Taxes and Contributions* by William Petty (1623–87), economist, scientist and philosopher, in which he mentions 'Land Taxe' as a means of raising revenue.

1692. Amongst a package of other taxes on personal estate, movable goods and income from public office, a Land Tax was introduced (which astonishingly endured until 1963). Initially this tax was based on annual rental values, but after the first valuation no more were carried out. From 1698, quotas based on acreages at the 1692 values were established for each county and remained fixed thereafter. Consequently, the amount collected diminished progressively from 35% of total revenue at the start to 17% in the 1790s and 11% by the 1820s. By 1733 that part of the tax on personal income and moveable goods had proved too difficult to collect and was largely abandoned, so the tax became almost entirely based on the revenue from land. The tax became gradually overshadowed by other taxes but continued into the 20th century, eventually raising no more than the cost of collection. It was finally abolished in 1963.[1]

1758. Publication of *Tableau Economique* by François Quesnay (1694–1774), French economist, physician to Louis 15th and co-founder of the Physiocrats. The Physiocrats considered that all wealth was derived from the agrarian production of land and proposed a single tax on land only.

1775. Lecture on land reform delivered to the Newcastle Philosophical Society by Thomas Spence (1750–1814), pamphleteer and revolutionary. In his lecture he proposed the formation of parish corporations that would collect the economic rent of land in place of all other tolls and taxes.

1776. Publication of *The Wealth of Nations* by Adam Smith (1723–90), political economist and philosopher. Smith is generally considered to be the father of classical economics. In his book he advocates the taxing of ground rents.

1781. Publication of *An Essay on the Right of Property in Land* by William Ogilvie, (1736–1819), Scottish landowner and classical scholar. In his treatise Ogilvie states, 'The gross amount of property in land is the fittest subject of taxation.'

1796. Publication of *Agrarian Justice* by Thomas Paine (1737–1809), political theorist and revolutionary. In his pamphlet he wrote, 'Every proprietor owes to the community a ground rent for the land which he holds.'

1817. Publication of *On the Principles of Political Economy and Taxation* by David Ricardo (1772–1823). Ricardo is credited with identifying the principle of the Economic Rent, or the Law of Rent.

1848. Publication of *The Principles of Political Economy* by John Stuart Mill (1806–73), political economist and philosopher. In Book 5, Chapter 2, he describes the benefits landlords gain from rents in which, 'They grow richer, as it were in their sleep, without working, risking or economising.'

1879. Publication of *Progress and Poverty* by Henry George (1839–97), American economist and social philosopher. In his book George finally pulls together all the threads and comprehensively explains an economic system based on land value taxation, which will become the definitive work and will give rise to a worldwide movement.

1891. After the publication of his book, George's ideas were adopted by the British Liberal party whose policies were formulated and declared each year by the National Liberal Foundation. This was a precursor to the manifestos adopted later by all parties, and an acknowledgement that party members should be allowed to influence policies. Meeting in Newcastle in 1891, the Liberals published their Newcastle Programme, which included rating reform and a 'just taxation of land values and ground rents.' This was the first declaration of LVT as a policy by any British political party.[2]

Smith, Ricardo and Mill were the founders of what came to be known as classical economics, in which land was considered an essential factor of production along with labour and capital and the phenomenon of economic rent was acknowledged. In the late 19th and early 20th century the neoclassical school of economics arose, in which land became considered as a part of capital, and so the significance of land became obscured (see Appendix 1). This neoclassical school still dominates current economic theory but is now being challenged by many independent free-thinking economists.[3]

4.2 20th Century History

Henry George's influence was extensive after the publication of *Progress and Poverty*. His ideas attracted many progressive thinkers and politicians of the time, not least of which was a young Winston Churchill, who became a Liberal MP in 1904. However, the forces of landed vested interests also recognised the threat to their power base and were always able to defeat attempts to introduce any system of LVT. The 'People's Budget' of the Liberal government of 1909 included LVT, but it was defeated by the Lords, most of whom were landlords. Any further progress was curtailed by the onset of World War One, and then by the return of a Conservative administration in 1922. During the first four decades of the 20th century numerous attempts to introduce LVT were made by local authorities, or, at the national level, through private member's bills, by Liberal or Labour MPs. These attempts are well documented in the book *Land Value Taxation in Britain* by Owen Connellan.[4]

It was during this period that the Liberals became displaced by the ascendant Labour party—which had always supported the idea of LVT. In a further attempt, in 1931, the Labour Chancellor Philip Snowden included LVT in his March budget and it became Part 3 of the following Finance Act. But in the subsequent Conservative dominated coalition, elected in October, the measure was repealed. In 1938 the Labour MP Herbert Morrison attempted to introduce a site-value rating bill for the London County area, but this was defeated again by a Conservative led majority. Events were then overtaken by the advent of World War Two. After the war LVT became forgotten in the new Labour government's enthusiasm for the Town and Country Planning Act of 1947, which was indeed a necessary and progressive measure. To it we owe the fact that England remains largely a green and pleasant land, but it did not deal sufficiently with the unearned gains to be made through land ownership. Also, many members of the Labour party held on to the belief that nationalisation was the best solution. In his book *The New Enclosure*, Brett Christophers quotes the then chancellor Hugh Dalton celebrating the fact that 'We are moving towards the nationalisation of the land.'[5]

However, the government was aware that large gains could now be made through speculation and the possibilities of 'planning gain', but the development charge that was part of the act was insufficient to capture the betterment gains for which it was intended. The landlords simply held on to their land and did not develop it, awaiting a change of government, which arrived in 1951, and which duly repealed the charge.

The manifestation of planning gain was not something new; it appeared long before the 1947 Act. In his book *The People's Rights*, Winston Churchill reported that immediately after the decision to go ahead with the Manchester Ship Canal in 1885 the prices of the necessary land to be purchased for the project rose by five or six times, to the exclusive benefit of the local landowners, who contributed nothing to the scheme.[6]

The Conservative government took the matter further in protecting the interests of the landowners. In 1961 they introduced the Land Compensation Act, which was part of legislation required to compensate property owners in the event of compulsory purchase. Within the act, section 5 provided for additional compensation for the loss of speculative 'hope' value due to anticipated future increases in land values.

The next Labour government introduced the Land Commission Act Betterment Levy in 1967, designed to recoup, for the government, a share of the land-value increase arising from a permission being granted, but this was ritually abolished by the succeeding Conservative government in 1970. In a further move, in 1975, the third post-war Labour government brought in the Community Land Act, followed by the Development Land Tax in 1976. However, none of these measures really encompassed the underlying principle of LVT, which is the *continuous* collection of the economic rent for the public purse.

Throughout the whole post-war period, the inability to understand the real significance of land values is evident in the various attempts at taxing 'betterment gains.' The capital gains tax (introduced in 1967) serves only to obscure the importance of land values; it is applied to all property, including art, antiques and cars, and principal homes are exempt. It is beset with complex exemptions and conditions, and in any case only applies once, at the moment of sale.

It has long been recognised that taxpayer-funded infrastructure increases land values, the benefits of which go to private landlords in the form of higher rents and property values. In order to help finance the costs of infrastructure related to particular sites under development, the Town and Country Planning Act of 1990 incorporated a 'Section 106 Agreement' (also known as Planning Obligation), which enabled local authorities to recoup some of the costs from the developer in exchange for the planning consent. However, this was a matter of negotiation and included such items as the provision of affordable housing as part of the deal.

Because of perceived deficiencies in this system the Town and Country Planning Act of 2010 included a new Community Infrastructure Levy (CIL) based on a fixed tariff schedule, so avoiding the uncertainties of negotiation. At the time, the CIL was considered simpler and more transparent for raising funds, which could be used over a general area, whereas Section 106 was more site-specific and was seen as more suitable for negotiating the levels of affordable housing. Both systems could be used in tandem, but care had to be taken to avoid any duplication of charges.

All of the above attempts at land value capture (LVC) due to taxpayer-created value, suffer from the same fatal flaw: they were and are dependent on single events; they do not have the continuity that is necessary for any useful system of raising revenue through taxation. They show a disregard of the continuity implicit in the underlying Law of Rent revealed 200 years previously by David Ricardo.

In recent years, the term 'land value capture' has been more commonly adopted amongst politicians and economists to describe the process of recouping the increases in land values for the public benefit. Some economists see it as an umbrella term that includes the land value tax. But for me the opposite is more accurate; it is the land value tax that incorporates land value capture. In most discussions on land value capture the main concern is with capturing the increase in land values due to publicly funded infrastructure, usually short-term single projects. But as I explain in Chapter 5 there are other causes that affect land values, which are permanent. Also, the discussions are always about increases of land value, never about decreases. The land value tax takes into account all of these contingencies.

Various ideas for land value capture have been proposed in recent years, which include:

Tax Increment Financing (TIF)

This is a system of land value capture relating to specific infrastructure projects, whereby a proportion of the resulting increase in property values can be recouped by the local authority to finance the project. It has been employed (not without controversy) in the US[7] and is supported in the UK by Centre for Cities, an organisation which represents the interests of mainly provincial cities.

Community Land Auctions (CLAs)

Using this mechanism, land parcels which come up for sale and which gain in value through planning consent for development can be auctioned to the highest bidder; the local authority taking a proportion of the proceeds. This system has been advocated by Tim Leunig of the think tank Centre Forum.[8]

The TIF and CLA systems both recognize the significance of increased land values, but still only apply to one-off events.

The Mansion Tax

The proposed Mansion Tax arose as a consequence of the excessive increases of house prices, especially before the economic collapse of 2008. As was explained earlier, the houses themselves do not change in any material way. What changes is the value of the sites upon which they are located. The Mansion Tax is an attempt to recoup some of this increase of value by imposing an annual tax of 1% on houses exceeding £2 m in value. Unfortunately, as with the current council tax, it makes no distinction between building value and site value. It has been pointed out that the same end result could be achieved by simply extending the existing council tax bands, the valuation basis being the same. As with TIF and CLA, a Mansion Tax would be automatically incorporated in any comprehensive system of land value taxation.

A report by the House of Commons Committee on Land Value Capture published in September 2018 recorded that both section 106 and CIL were in need of improvement.[9] CIL was reported as inflexible and only suited to smaller developments in high value areas, so it was not much used by local authorities outside London and the South East. Commenting on section 106, one participant asserted that, 'it was not fit for capturing land values.' Several participants felt that where negotiations were concerned, many local authorities were no match for more skilful private developers. In an attempt to remedy these defects, the final recommendations included further supplementary systems: LIT, (Local Infrastructure Tariff), which applied to all developments, and SIT (Strategic Infrastructure Tariff), which is similar to the mayoral CIL employed for Crossrail in London. These proposals, of course, only applied to the increase of values due to infrastructure.

One has the rather depressing sense that this proliferation of ever more schemes for capturing land value are yet another demonstration of an inability (or unwillingness?) to recognise the underlying causes. A straightforward land value tax would sweep away all these ingenious but ultimately unworkable schemes with a system that comprehensively includes all forms of LVC, one which is continuous and takes into account all the causes of land value increase not simply those due to infrastructure.

CHAPTER 5

ASPECTS OF LVT

To prove legal title to land, one must trace it back to the man who stole it.

David Lloyd George (1863–1945): British Prime Minister, 1916–1922

5.1 Causes of Land Value

In chapter 2 the relationship between urban land values and location is shown to be fundamental, but within that context it is worth noting how land in general or sites in particular may acquire value. The primary causes affecting land value are:

1. Natural advantages
2. Infrastructure
3. Population Density (agglomeration)
4. The Planning System
5. Security.

It's important to note that, where the causes of land value are concerned, there is a big difference between urban land and agricultural/rural land. With urban land, causes two to five certainly apply but the first cause, natural advantages, is considerably diminished if not totally absent. With agricultural land, natural advantages are of course of primary importance, while infrastructure is less so, and population density of no significance. Rural land values are predominately due to the providence of nature, whereas urban land values are essentially man-made.

The influence of the planning system has an effect on both urban and rural land values; a rural site, if designated for urban residential use, will gain enormously in value at the stroke of a planner's pen. It is this artificial 'planning gain' that has long been the subject of much discussion. Natural advantages are exceptional in that they are a given; they are relatively unchanging. All the other causes are man-made and are subject to variation.

Where infrastructure is concerned, it is usually assumed that any addition will give rise to a corresponding increase in land values, and this is generally the case, but there are situations where its introduction may reduce land values, for instance to properties adjacent to a new bypass or under the flight path of a new airport runway. Also, where planning is concerned, residential property values may well decline where permission is granted for some adjacent industrial or commercial project. However, the general trend for land values to rise due to any or all the above factors still holds true.

Rather than the value of a site being due to any one cause, it is more likely to be a combination of causes that go towards the demand to occupy that particular site. One thing is certain: the demand for a site determines its value and in the urban context that value varies according to its location. Adam Smith, in a chapter on the location of housing, noted that:

> Ground rents are generally highest in the capital, and in those particular parts of it where there happens to be the greatest demand for houses, whatever be the reason for that demand, whether for trade and business, for pleasure and society, or for mere vanity and fashion.[1]

1. Natural Advantages

These causes are in place at the outset as they are provided by nature and simply need to be recognised in order to be exploited. The earliest settlers would establish themselves on the most fertile land with a fresh water source, or at the tidal limit, at the confluence of rivers or where known underground resources were easily accessible. The benefits of natural advantage are more evident in an agrarian situation, or in an industrial context where it is a question of the exploitation of underground resources. In this latter case the effect on land values is indirect, as I explain in the next chapter under Industrial Land Values. With later urban development these natural advantages became overtaken by the man-made advantages of infrastructure and agglomeration.

2. Infrastructure

As the community grows, the need for communal facilities increases proportionately. In the earliest stages these requirements are pretty basic, a village well, a schoolhouse, a bridge. Proximity to these facilities increases land values. In the later, more developed community, the requirements become more advanced: sewerage systems, street lighting, water, gas and electricity services, transport systems etc. All of these facilities may be described as infrastructure, which falls into two types according to how it is financed—publicly or privately. Public infrastructure is financed and maintained through taxation. Private infrastructure is financed through private investment capital and maintained out of profits from charging for the service. In either case proximity of a site to any of these facilities would normally increase its value. However, there are exceptions to this rule, as mentioned previously. Where the land values are adversely affected by new infrastructure, any land-value based tax would be proportionately reduced.

In Britain in the 19th century, the railways were a highly lucrative private investment but were eventually rendered uneconomic with the advent of the internal combustion engine and the growth of road transport. However, having become an integral part of the economic structure of the country they had to be nationalised, in 1948, to maintain the service, on which the country had become dependent. The railways could not be allowed to die away, as had the canal system when superseded by the railways. The subsequent attempt at re-privatisation has never really worked, and the railway system is still heavily subsidised by the taxpayer. Those who have consistently profited from the railways throughout the whole period are the landlords close to the stations, whose property values have constantly increased.

Also part of infrastructure are services such as those provided by the NHS and the school system. When buying a house, parents will pay extra to be in the catchment area of a good school. This increases the economic pressure locally, which is reflected immediately in higher house prices.

3. Population Density (agglomeration)

The simple fact of population presence increases land values. Where all other factors remain unchanged, any population increase will increase the economic pressure within a community. Those who move into a new community need not be active 'producers'; they may do so simply for residential purposes, but no matter; their mere presence will increase the demand for goods and services, and those who provide the goods and services will prosper and compete for the best sites on which to operate, which will inevitably increase the site values. If the new residents are also working elsewhere within the community, their work will add to the co-operative surplus and the overall wealth of the community. Increases of population due to immigrants willing and able to work will always increase the general level of prosperity. In his book *The Future of Capitalism*, Paul Collier notes,

> The gains from agglomeration are generated by interactions between masses of people, and so they are a collective achievement that benefits everyone.[2]

Agricultural and industrial land are exceptions in this context. As shown in the diagrams in Chapter 2, the agglomeration effect is only significant in an urban context. The 'agglomeration' of a hundred farms over a vast area would not produce an agrarian economic centre due to location. The location value of farmland would vary only according to proximity to markets, abattoirs, grain storage facilities etc.

4. The Planning System

The planning system represents a massive but necessary interference with the natural development of urban land values. Unrestrained organic growth gave rise to the chaotic squalor of the great industrial cities of the 19th century, and in the 20th century, to the urban sprawl and ribbon developments of the inter-war years; house builders simply developed on each side of existing roads; the easiest option for them. This was seen as a wasteful and inefficient use of land, and attempts were made to bring it under control.

The Housing and Town Planning Act of 1909 was the first of a series of measures that culminated in the 1947 Town and Country Planning Act, which introduced the requirement of planning permission for any development, in particular for any proposed change of use. This gave rise to the phenomenon of 'planning gain', where a change of use permission could significantly increase the value of a site, with this increase accruing to the benefit of the landholder.

In 1955 the protective 'green belt' zones were introduced around major city conurbations, so magnifying the issue of planning gain, when a site was re-zoned.

Where land values are concerned, the old natural organic growth at least provided a comparatively smooth transition between different use values, whereas the imposition of zoning introduced very abrupt changes of value on either side of an artificial boundary. On the drawing board, planners may re-allocate an area for a different use or extend a boundary and so alter the potential values of the sites affected.

The differences of use-value vary considerably. Between say light industrial and retail uses the difference may not be great, but where it involves re-zoning of rural land previously within the green belt, for residential development, the change can create enormous differences—by as much as 275 times.[3] This betterment gain is partially redeemed under the present Community Infrastructure Levy, depending on the tariff rate set by the local authority, which is known in advance by the developer. This system is arguably better than the previous 106 agreement, where the payment was negotiated, but it is still only a one-off payment and does not take into account ongoing rental values in the future.

Under an LVT system I would suggest a more productive process. For example, when a change of green belt zoning for housing development is intended, the local authority could compulsorily purchase the land, close to existing use value, with compensation for disturbance to the farmer/landowner. The land could then be sold on the open market for residential development to the highest bidder. The developer would buy the land in the full knowledge of the future LVT obligation. In this way the farmer would get a fair price plus compensation, the local authority would get the best competitive price with an assured tax revenue base in the future, and the developer would acquire a valuable site at his own price. Any need to appease local residents with particular amenities could be financed from the increased tax revenue.

5. Security

All communities require security. The vast majority of people throughout the world want a situation where they are able to live and work peacefully in a secure environment. Except during the period of the 'troubles' in Northern Ireland, in the UK we have rather taken for granted the security we enjoy. Lack of security and the rule of law affects the economic circumstances of any community. There are now various official websites showing heat-maps of high crime areas, both nationally and locally. Absence of security discourages inward immigration and investment, impedes productive activity and reduces any desire of outsiders to locate in the community. This of course lowers land values.

An interesting case was in Rio de Janeiro where, from 2008, the authorities conducted a policy of 'pacification' in certain slum *favelas*, which had become crime-ridden no-go areas. The police moved in and systematically cleared out the drug-pushers and criminal gangs and maintained permanent street patrols. Once the pacification was seen to be successful, residents and traders moved back in, with the result that property values increased rapidly.[4] Some favelas were in good locations with stunning views over the ocean but had lost their economic value due to the lack of security.

5.2 Ownership of Land

The exercise of power in economic affairs invariably derives from ownership: whoever owns an enterprise or organisation will decide on the laws and procedures that govern it. Whoever owns the elements of production will set the conditions that lead to that production. This applies particularly to land, which is one of the two original elements of wealth creation, the other being labour. Except in slave states, it has always been accepted that we own our own bodies and our own labour, but we do not all own our own land, or perhaps what is more pertinent, the access to land.

One of the prime causes of poverty began with the original acts of dispossession, the separation of labour from access to the land by those who claimed exclusive possession—usually by force of arms. This original expropriation has been the cause of much subsequent poverty, making men beholden to the owners of one of the two components of wealth creation, with only their labour to bargain with. The landholders held the whip hand and drove a hard bargain, resulting in the return to labour, in the form of wages, being forced down to subsistence levels. In his book *The Possibility of Progress*, Mark Braund sets it out clearly:

> Those who own land are best placed; those who own capital are well placed, but those who only

have their labour to sell can only expect minimal reward.[5]

The great advantage to the landlords was that, by default, they had control over large numbers of dispossessed labourers, whereas the labourers were disorganised individuals, set in competition with each other for the choice of either working for a pittance or starvation. Despite peasants' revolts and Luddite retaliations, this unbalanced master/worker relationship did not change until the realisation dawned on the working people that there was power in numbers—if properly organised; this gave rise to the early trade union movement. But even the revolutions that took place in France and Russia did not change the basic dispensation, where those who held the land also held the reins of economic power.

As was observed by Andrew MacLaren, the independent Labour MP for Burslem in the 1930s and a strong LVT advocate, 'Revolutions take place in the mind, not in the streets.'[6]

The improvement in workers' conditions was hard won over many years, and as with all transfers of power, it was never surrendered, it always had to be wrested. In-work poverty was the norm for the lower classes for many centuries and was only remedied slowly through extending the voting franchise and with the advent of organised labour.

Eventually, the state welfare system, although an unfortunate necessity, became the main source of remediation. But throughout its existence the welfare system has struggled to measure up to the demands made upon it. Even now, after more than a hundred years of the existence of the welfare state, in-work poverty is returning. Alleviation of poverty is of course a necessary measure, but it is never a substitute for the elimination of the original cause; the expropriation of the land and the channelling of the economic rent into private pockets.

In his book *Silent Theft*, David Bollier comments: 'We know at some level that nature cannot really be owned.'[7] Also, in the book *Land Value Taxation Around the World*, Robert Keall adds, 'Private enterprise must not include private ownership of the natural elements of life.'[8] But when the possibility of material gain is at stake it is not always convenient for land to be seen as part of nature.

The idea that land may be owned is very well entrenched with most people in the developed world. Even those who do not own land and have very little prospect of doing so subscribe to the idea. To question this belief would seem perverse to say the least. Indeed, the even stronger assertion that land *must* be owned is almost equally accepted, especially of course amongst landowners. But as Andy Wightman points out in his aptly titled book *The Poor Had No Lawyers*, 'at a certain level all land tenure systems are made up— fictions that are true only for as long as people believe in them.'[9]

In England land ownership has a long history: After the Norman conquest, the nobles who had supported the king were rewarded with estates of land for their loyal service. The fact that the king had no right to gift this land carried no weight; no one argued with the king. Kings would also lease or sell off land to finance their frequent wars. In Shakespeare's play, *Richard II*, scene one of act two is about a visit by the king to his uncle, the dying John of Gaunt, who laments the selling off of leases by the king to finance his campaign in Ireland; he makes the telling accusation, 'Landlord of England thou art now, not king.'

The title of this book is taken from the famous 'sceptre'd isle' speech, which stirs the hearts of all English patriots, but the ending of which tells a very different story:

> This land of such dear souls, this dear, dear land,
> Dear for her reputation through the world,
> Is now leased out—I die pronouncing it.
> Like to a tenement or pelting farm:
> England, bound in with the triumphant sea
> Whose rocky shore beats back the envious siege of
> wat'ry Neptune,
> Is now bound in with shame.
> With inky blots and rotten parchment bonds,
> That England, that was wont to conquer others
> Hath made a shameful conquest of itself.
> Ah, would the scandal vanish with my life
> How happy then were my ensuing death!

The later enclosures were no more than blatant acts of theft of the land from the peasants, and throughout these times there were always lawyers willing to legitimise these acts of theft with 'legal' documents granting titles. These were passed down through the generations, gaining in validity simply through the veneration bestowed by antiquity. Wightman notes, 'The role of the law has historically been to serve the interest of those in power.'[10] He also notes that the purpose of the Law of Prescription introduced in Scotland in 1617 was 'to legitimise in the eyes of the law the theft of Church lands.'[11] The benefit to be gained was of course the economic rent, which accrued as a matter of course to the landowner and which Henry George later described as continuous robbery:

> This robbery is not like the robbery of a horse or a sum of money, that ceases with the act. It is a fresh and continuous robbery, that goes on every day and every hour. [12]

It is a sad fact that there has always been a minority within the legal profession that have colluded for centuries in perpetuating an injustice that, apart from times of war, has arguably brought more misery and hardship to a great many ordinary people than any other single cause, and continues to do so to the present day. Certainly, the majority of lawyers remain true to the ideal of justice through good laws, but there are others who have used their skills, for no little reward, in the interests of wealthy and powerful clients.[13]

But from the point of view of those who advocate LVT, the ownership of land is not the main point; it is the ownership of the economic rent of land that matters. Of course, these two aspects are connected but in his wisdom, Henry George recognised that to avoid conflict with the great landowners, the two could be treated separately. The ownership of the land could continue, but not the ownership of the economic rent.

> Let the landholders have, if you please, all that the possession of the land would give them in the absence of the rest of the community. But rent, the creation of the whole community, necessarily belongs to the whole community.[14]

However, George also recognised that with a 100% LVT landowners would have no financial interest in continued ownership, so to avoid the land being neglected or abandoned he allowed that a proportion should be left to the landlord as a payment for good stewardship.[15]

The notion of landownership has a very powerful hold in the US. One reason for this is the influence of the English political philosopher John Locke (1632–1704). He had a particular view of private property in land, and strongly influenced the American Founding Fathers in drawing up the constitution. In his Second Treatise of Government, published in 1689, he proposed that work applied to land was a qualification for ownership. This view coloured a great deal of thinking on the issue of private property, in particular that of land, and gave rise to much debate, which continues to this day. The critical paragraph in his treatise is reproduced here in full:

> Though the Earth, and all inferior Creatures be common to all Men, yet every Man has a Property in his own Person. This no Body has any Right to but himself. The Labour of his Body, and the Work of his Hands, we may say are properly his. Whatsoever then he removes out of the State that Nature hath provided, and left it in, he hath

mixed his Labour with, and joined to it something that is his own, and thereby makes it his Property. It being by him removed from the common state nature placed it, it hath by his labour something annexed to it that excludes the common right of other Men. For this Labour being the unquestionable Property of the Labourer, no Man but he can have a right to what that is once joined to, at least where there is enough, and as good left in common for others.[16]

Although Locke was right in making the connection between ownership and work, or more precisely the ownership of the wealth created through work, he was wrong to extend that ownership to the basic resource from which the wealth was created.

Most would accept that no matter for how long or how hard our fishermen have worked, though they are entitled to ownership of their catch, they are not entitled to ownership of the ocean, or even a part of it.

However, Locke qualified his view with a proviso in the very last line—'where there is enough and as good left in common for others.' And it is this proviso that has thrown doubt on the theory and left room for much debate ever since. However, his writings carried great weight thereafter and became a primary justification for land ownership. Quite possibly it influenced the American Homestead Act of 1862, which granted the early settlers not only ownership but also the security they wanted and deserved due to their hard work.

In a paper published in 1968, 'The Tragedy of the Commons', the American biologist Garret Hardin consolidated the belief that land had to be owned—either privately or by the state. His theory became very influential amongst economists, especially with the neo-liberals, who embraced the idea of private ownership. It provided them with a further moral justification. Hardin's theory was later debunked by the Nobel economics laureate Elinor Ostrom, but not before it had gained widespread popularity.[17]

In Britain, the notion of the ownership of land—public or private—is now virtual holy writ with most people, and the idea is naturally reinforced by the increase in the number of homeowners, especially in the last 50 years. One might say that land ownership has become democratised with the increase of homeownership. The land is seen as an integral part of one's home, one's property, and any attempt to alter that status is strongly resisted as an attack on one's private property. But at the same time the same people can be more amenable to the idea of the non-ownership of other natural resources, such as minerals in the ground, fish in the sea, water resources and so on—these are perhaps less personal than one's own back garden. It is highly unlikely that this view about land will change, and as Henry George pointed out, it does not need to for the collection of the economic rent. It is from this point of view that LVT becomes practicable.

There is no need to alter the existing arrangement of land ownership, providing the economic rent is duly surrendered. This separation of land ownership from land rent must be understood and accepted by the general population, but therein lies the difficulty. A great deal of this book is about explaining this distinction and thereby providing a justification for LVT, but in this process it is worth considering the notion of ownership in general, apart from that concerning land.

If we accept that all (physical) wealth arises from work carried out on land (all natural resources), the wealth so produced rightfully belongs to whoever has carried out the work—physical or mental. It is the work element not the land element that provides the claim to ownership. The land element is provided by nature and is fixed; the work element is provided through human effort and is variable. One may say that the individual ownership of wealth due to work is legitimate but the individual ownership of land or any other natural resource is not.

In July of 2013, in a High Court ruling over a dispute on fish quotas, Justice Cranston ruled that, 'No-one can own the fish of the sea.'[18] There is the ring of truth about this statement. But if we were to extend this idea to the ownership of all natural resources, then they could only be owned collectively by the whole human race. Everyone on the planet would in effect become a shareholder in whatever wealth resulted from the exploitation of these resources. They would therefore be entitled to a dividend from any surplus after the return to labour had been deducted. Although this would be impractical to administer under current circumstances, it would be fair in principle.

As an illustration of this: In January 2019, $3.1 million was paid for a 278 kg bluefin tuna in the Tokyo fish market.[19] Disregarding for the moment the deductions due to wastage and labour, the total value of this one fish divided between the 7.8 billion humans on the planet would be about 0.04 US cents each. This might not sound very much, but in 2018 the world catch of tuna amounted to about 5 million tonnes.[20] At an average dockside price of say $2 per kg the total sale value would be $10 billion. Deducting say 50% for labour and processing costs this would still leave $5 billion which, divided by 7.8, would provide an annual dividend of 64 US cents to everyone on the planet. This return is for tuna only. Add to this amount the returns for whales and the other sea fish and the total would result in an amount very beneficial to those in the developing world living on $2 a day. This dividend is the equivalent of a rent due to ownership. It is similar to the rent paid to a private landlord for the use of a property. One could extend the above example to include the returns arising from all the world's other natural resources, where no one is the owner but everyone is a shareholder—a concept that is the basis for resource rents (see Resource Rents, below).

Land is considered to be the primary resource. Other than those who depend for their livelihood and sustenance from the sea, we can live without eating fish or burning coal, but we cannot live without land, and the collection of the resource rent of land, the economic rent, goes to whoever controls the land—the private owner or the government representing the people—but it hinges very much on our view of ownership.

There is no justification for any claim to ownership of land through any natural law. The land title documents drawn up over the centuries, are no more than legalisations of original acts of appropriation or theft. It could be argued that we who are proud owners of the site upon which our houses stand are receivers of stolen property, at least where the site is concerned. We are of course able to deflect this accusation by producing our 'legal' documents. We can also take some comfort in numbers: some 60% of all homes in the UK at present are owner-occupied. Additionally, it is reassuring to know that Winston Churchill, that great LVT advocate, said: 'We do not want to punish the landlord, we want to alter the law'.[21]

And so the situation will no doubt continue for the foreseeable future, but, as has been said, the critical issue is not the ownership of the land but the ownership of the economic rent. In a stable society people require security, both for their legitimate property and also for the continuing use of the land they occupy—the security of tenure. Security of tenure can always be provided through a leasehold system which sets out the terms and conditions of occupation, and where the freeholder is the government.

Such a system has operated successfully for many years in Hong Kong, where one of the conditions for leaseholders is the surrender of an annual ground rent (a quasi LVT) to the government.* However imperfect, it works well for Hong Kong and enables other taxes to be kept low. The system is described very well in Andrew

---

* It should be added that the government of Hong Kong, as the freeholder, derives more revenue from the sale of the leases by auction at regular intervals.

Purves' book *No Debt, High Growth, Low Tax*.[22] A similar system operates in Singapore, and whatever deficiencies there may be in those two states with civil freedoms and wealth distribution, Hong Kong and Singapore are recognised as highly successful and prosperous city states; they came first and second respectively in the World Economic Freedom Index in 2019.[23] They are both countries which show how even a modified form of LVT is effective in raising revenue.

Various partial forms of LVT are practised beneficially in many other countries including Denmark, Estonia, Taiwan, Australia and the USA. In these countries it makes little difference whether the land is owned privately or by the government. As long as the land rent is collected by the government, the system can work effectively.

5.3 Resource Rents

Amongst economists it is generally understood that the word 'land' includes all natural resources, all gifts of nature, natural forests, wildlife, minerals in the ground, fish in the sea etc. This definition raises the question of ownership, exploitation rights and also the concept of resource rents. Justice Cranston's ruling on fish could apply equally to all natural resources.

It is debatable whether land is actually a natural resource. Food, air and water are not seen as resources but as the very essentials of life; land is just as essential. Resources may be considered as necessary for civilised life but not for life itself; human beings existed and flourished, however primitively, before the discovery of minerals, coal or oil. However, for the purpose of this book land is treated as a natural resource (see Chapter 13, Definitions), if not the most fundamental of all resources. The questions raised here are about the control or ownership of these resources and who should receive the benefits.

The basic principles that govern land value taxation may be applied equally to all natural resources. As all natural resources are a gift of nature they cannot be owned, not even by governments or nations. Public custodianship may be accepted by general consent as a practical administrative necessity, but a wise government would be careful to distinguish this from ownership.[24]

If ownership of a natural resource is to be allowed, then the benefits derived may be equally claimed by all human beings on the planet, who could be seen as the collective beneficiaries. This raises the issue of the practicality of determining such an equal shareholding. This problem has been resolved historically by the convention of accepting that each nation (or tribe) may claim ownership of those resources over which it has territorial control; so natural forests, minerals, water, oil or fish in the sea are allowed to be claimed by mutual unwritten consent amongst all nations.

Fishing of the open seas beyond territorial limits has always been seen as open to all; inside these limits disputes are commonplace. This dispensation has obtained throughout history (despite periods of warfare) but is now coming under some strain with the exponential growth of world population, the rise of international corporations and the acceleration of globalisation. Claims for the ownership of natural resources are now put forward by private companies on the strength of their new control, not of territory, but over the economies of the erstwhile owners. The private economies of corporations are now often greater than those of the host countries, so they are able to dictate the terms of gaining access to resources. These developments have given rise to a new awareness of the value of the world's natural resources and the issue of ownership.

The principle guiding resource rents, is that no individual or organisation has the right to appropriate or exercise control over any gift of nature without recognising a debt to society in the form of an appropriate payment. Such payment may be described as a 'resource rent'. A land value tax is a similar payment, which is not strictly a tax but rather a payment to society for the beneficial occupation or use of a site. In a system of private land ownership this payment is made to the landlord. In his book, *The Corruption of Economics*, co-authored with Mason Gaffney, Fred Harrison makes the interesting point, 'The tenant does not claim that he is being taxed when he pays rent to the private landlord!'[25]

However, where LVT is concerned, it is important to distinguish between rural land and urban land. Rural land may have value already due to natural circumstances, and this may be increased through directly applied work. The three-dimensional resources of coal, oil, fish etc. are tangible physical resources that require work to convert them into useable wealth.* Urban land, however, requires no such work; it simply has to be there. With urban land, what is being considered is a two-dimensional area on the surface of the earth that has enhanced value because of its location within a man-made agglomeration.

Where natural resources are concerned, the increase of land value due to agglomeration does not apply; the natural resource may be remote from the location that benefits from its exploitation. The increased land values in Aberdeen are due to remote 'work on land' a hundred miles away in the North Sea. For all these reasons it is more appropriate for the wealth derived from natural resources to be taxed through a licensing or leasing system, whereby a private entrepreneur is granted a lease to exploit the natural resource for an agreed return over an agreed period to the controlling government—a resource rental.

Another option is for the government to invite companies to bid for a contract to carry out the extraction. Whoever came in with the best rental offer would get the contract for a fixed period.

---

* An exception has to be made for the electromagnetic spectrum, which, as an intangible resource, requires no work for extraction but only for exploitation. It is undoubtedly a resource from which a revenue may be derived for its use. In his book *The Stewardship Economy*, Julian Pratt notes that in the year 2000 the British government received over £22 billion from private companies in payment for 20-year licences granting access to the radio spectrum.[26]

CHAPTER 6

LAND VALUES

An acre in Middlesex is better
than a principality in Utopia.

Lord Macaulay (1800–59):
Historian, politician and poet

6.1 Industrial Land Values

In the explanation of Chapter 2 you may wonder why
there is no mention of industrial land. This is because
there is a big distinction to be made between heavy and
light industry. For the purpose of the explanation, light-
industrial land comes under the heading of 'commercial'.
Heavy-industrial land is somewhat anomalous in that,
where land values are concerned, it does not follow
the same pattern of development as for other forms of
economic activity.

The evolution of heavy-industry land values are
perhaps better understood in a historical context.

In Britain, the earliest industrial activity was related
to the location of natural resources. The iron ore and
water power of South Yorkshire gave rise to the steel

industry. The wealth of South Wales was based on the rich coal seams. The coal, humid climate and soft water of South Lancashire gave rise to the cotton industry. But the steelworks, coalmines and cotton mills themselves did not increase the land values of the sites on which they were situated. On the contrary, these industries gave rise to what became blighted areas surrounded by slum housing which had the effect of depressing overall values. No doubt the simple presence of an increased population added to the overall economic pressure, but the benefit of that was manifested elsewhere and not in the industrial area itself. The very activity of mining, for instance, depressed the value of the site and the surrounding areas. The mining rights and the mining installation may have had very high value to the owner or any potential buyer, but the location value of the site due to agglomeration was negligible.

Areas previously engaged in heavy industry do not generally have high land values. They are located at or beyond the urban agglomeration, where land values are low or marginal. The wealth created from these activities is spent elsewhere. The coal, iron and cotton industries of 19th century Britain created great wealth, reflected in the growing size and prosperity of the provincial cities; in the business districts and select residential areas where the wealth was spent. It was in these separate and sometimes distant areas that land values increased; on the site of the industry itself the surrounding land values remained low, reflecting the reduced circumstances of those that worked in the industry, but received only a meagre share of the wealth created. The bulk of the wealth went to the owners and shareholders.

Clearly, a land value tax in these locations would raise little revenue and would not reflect the revenue potential of an otherwise wealthy industry. So how should heavy industry be taxed?

I would suggest that a formula could be agreed between the government and representatives of the industry that, apart from any land value tax, would be based on company profits and shareholder dividends. This would reflect the real wealth of the company and its ability to pay. Where the extractive industries are concerned the best solution would be a licensing system as described in Chapter 5, Resource Rents.

Taking a more contemporary situation: A modern oil refinery may be of immense value as an essential piece of capital equipment and command a high resale price, but the site on which it stands may have originally had only low agricultural value. If the industry were to shut down, the installation would not only become a liability, but the land would not even have agricultural value.

In recent times, where industries have gone into decline or disappeared altogether, the abandoned 'brownfield' sites may be adjacent to or within a growing agglomeration and may therefore have high potential value for a different use, but they remain virtually unsaleable due to the cost of clearance and decontamination. With an LVT system, such sites could be purchased by the local authority, which would bear the cost of clearance and restoration. The site could then be sold for redevelopment under a different designation to the highest bidder, who would thereafter pay the appropriate land value tax.

6.2 Agricultural Land Values

In the explanation of Chapter 2, it can be seen that LVT is predominantly an urban rather than a rural tax, in the sense that by far the greater revenue would be derived from the former. Although rural land accounts for about 87% of Britain's total land area, it represents only about 5% of the total land value.[1] This means that rural land would contribute about 5% of the total LVT and urban land about 95%.

The primary difference between urban and rural land values is that urban land values are determined by location within a close-knit agglomeration of sites, each contributing to the economic pressure that gives rise to the increase of value. This significance of location does not apply within the rural situation, where sites are at some distance from any existing economic centre, and although they may be adjacent to each other, are far too large in area and diffuse to create any economic centre due to proximity.

As explained in Chapter 5, Causes of Land Value/ Population Intensity, there is no agglomeration effect where rural land is devoted entirely to farming. Agricultural land values are slight in comparison to urban land values, especially where large cities are concerned. Also, the variations in value due to location are much greater within an urban context.

The figures of Table 1 below, taken from the Valuation Office Agency Report for 2011, show the differences in values, in £ per acre, between agricultural and residential land for some typical areas in England.[2]

City/County	Residential land values per acre	Agricultural land values per acre	Res./Ag. multiple
Oxford Oxfordshire	£1.62 m. —	— £8,450	192
Leeds East Yorkshire	£0.55 m. —	— £6,252	88
Manchester Lancashire	£0.55 m. —	— £7,002	78
Leicester Leicestershire	£0.44 m. —	— £8,450	76

Table 1. Comparison of residential and adjacent agricultural land values for selected cities in England, 2011

(Source: Valuation Office Agency Report for 2011)

The fourth column in the table shows a multiple indicating how much more valuable the residential land is in the cities compared to the adjacent agricultural land. It is notable that the multiple for Oxford is far higher than the other three cities. This is entirely due to the much higher residential values. The multiple for Oxford is 2.5 times higher than that for Leicester, but the Oxfordshire and Leicestershire rural values are the same. It is likely that the higher residential values in Oxford are due to their proximity to London, but the 'London effect' does not apply where agricultural land is concerned. Whereas, urban values are determined by variations in location, agricultural values are determined mainly by variations in fertility, which are quite small by comparison. The best farmland (prime arable) is rarely more than double the price of the least valuable (poor grassland). Figures published by the estate agents Savills on farmland prices show that in 2011 the average prime arable land was selling for £7,000/acre and poor grassland at £3,500/acre.[3]

In a book on real estate investment in the US, Prof. Roger Brown presents an interesting diagram of land use rental values for a hypothetical city, in which he shows the breakdown of values and areas for different uses, ranging from commercial, light industrial, residential, heavy industrial through to agricultural.[4] His diagram bears a striking resemblance to Figure 12 in Chapter 2, which I show again here, in Figure 13, as a linear curve with the different zones indicated in similar proportions to those in Prof. Brown's diagram.

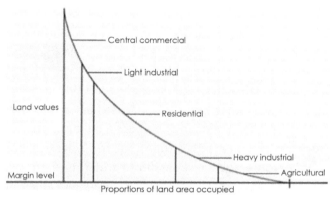

Fig.13   Comparison of land areas and values for different uses
within a typical developed city

It is notable that the largest land area is taken up by residential, and also that the agricultural zone values become marginal at the greatest distance from the centre. It is worth remembering that, where residential land is concerned, the LVT is a payment for occupation only, whereas all the other categories are for occupancy and productive use.

The diagram shows that where use values are concerned, agricultural land is always at the bottom of the hierarchy. Industrial land is always more valuable, and residential more valuable than both. In prime urban areas residential land can attain very high values. In London, in the Chelsea Barracks redevelopment scheme of 2008, the 12.8-acre site was sold for £959 million (£75 million/acre).[5] In London W1, in 2019, a residential plot was being offered for sale (without planning consent), at the rate of £576 million/acre.[6]

The point I'm making here is that there is a vast difference between urban and rural land values where LVT revenue potential is concerned.

As Table 1 shows, it would require 192 acres of Oxfordshire farmland to match the value of one acre of residential land in Oxford itself. In the central London example, a one-acre site would require an equivalent farm area of more than 68,000 acres.

So how might one resolve this taxation issue peculiar to rural land?

In any discussion of the economics of farming one has to take into account the subsidy system, which has been in place since World War Two. Rationing and subsidies were introduced during the war for understandable reasons during the emergency. To encourage production of food after the war, the 1947 Agriculture Act subsidised farmers in the form of price guarantees (food rationing continued until 1954). In 1973 Britain joined the European Union and came within the subsidy system of the Common Agricultural Policy (CAP). This policy encouraged all European farmers to produce more food than could be justified by the normal requirements of supply and demand and resulted in the infamous butter mountains and wine lakes.

Historically, the CAP emphasised direct subsidies for agricultural production. To reduce price distortion, the connection between subsidies and specific forms of production was removed. Instead, the Single Farm Payment was introduced in 2003, which subsidised farmers on a per hectare basis to comply with the World Trade Organisation agreements to reduce market-distorting subsidies and price controls. In Britain this encouraged large farmers to buy more land and gain the benefit of the increased subsidy. The policy encouraged landownership rather than food production and made life more difficult for those young would-be farmers who wanted to start farming.

Tenant farmers who receive subsidies pay most, if not all of the money to their landlords in rent. The number of tenant farmers has been in decline for decades. Rural land has become a speculative commodity, with constantly increasing land prices. This process could be reversed with the introduction of a land value tax, but it would also be necessary to eliminate the distortionary effect of subsidies. Julian Pratt notes that subsidies:

> burden the taxpayer and benefit the landowner by increasing the market rent and market value of land.[7]

Subsidies for any industry should only be used for some short-term emergency. Where they become permanent, they can only lead to a distortion of the natural economic balance.

As Britain has now left the European Union the CAP system will be replaced gradually by the provisions of the new Agriculture Act 2020 in which subsidies will continue but will be based more on environmental protection and restoration. Most of the subsidy money will still go to less than 30% of the farmers, who own about 70% of the land. The farmers will spend more of their time as park-keepers.

Introducing a land value tax in the rural situation would need to be part of a national system (as opposed to a local system) as explained in Chapter 3, Application of LVT. It would also need to be phased in over a transition period (of say 10 years) to avoid any disruption. The concurrent reduction of subsidies would be felt more by the small tenant farmer who in many cases has become dependent on them. The large farmer/landowner would also be affected, but only in the sense that the net worth of his land would fall. The introduction of LVT is conditional on a reduction of other taxes, which would benefit everyone in rural areas (see Chapter 3, Advantages of LVT). But to help the start-up tenant farmer in particular, perhaps the reduction could be applied directly as an allowance on their income tax payments, for a limited period until the situation normalised. In this way the farmer would be able to see the direct benefit to him of the change to LVT—in the way that I describe for the replacement of council tax in Chapter 7, Winners and Losers.

The small farmer would also be helped by a gradual reduction in land prices, as a consequence of LVT. The ideal would be no subsidies at all, with a fair return to the food-producing farmer, through a reduction in the costs of production and a higher return for his product.

According to the CAP Reform website[8] the farmers' share of the final shop prices for food in 1995 was 31%; the remaining 69% was divided between retailers, wholesalers and food processors. In 2011 the share was 21%, a drop of 10% in 16 years – and the trend continues. Farmers are the basic producers on whom the industry depends; they should get a fairer share and therefore be less dependent on subsidies. Farming has been subsidised since World War Two and has led many farmers to a state of dependency; not good for them or the taxpayers.

It's worth digressing slightly here to look at how we value food compared to other necessities:

It could be said that there are only three basic necessities for human survival: food, warmth and shelter. The need for food requires no explanation. Warmth is provided through clothing and heating, in whatever form. Shelter protects us from the elements and may range from anything between a luxury home to a simple tent; the homeless will seek shelter under a bridge. In the contemporary situation shelter is generally discussed under the catch-all heading of 'housing'. All three factors are considered essential although, of course, there may be luxury foods, luxury clothing and luxury housing, which may be seen as non-essential, but for the purpose of the following comparisons these distinctions are ignored. The figures shown are simply for the purpose of comparison—what proportion of household income is spent on these three essentials.

Housing is rather special in that it is necessary to distinguish between four social groups: outright owners, mortgagees, social renters and private renters. Outright owners are excluded; apart from maintenance their outlay is nil. All groups have to pay the council tax, but social renters may get a discount (which is means tested).

Bearing in mind that the average salary in 2021 was £29,600:[9]

Food.

According to the government data for the years between 2006–18, the percentage of household income spent on food depended on the level of income. The average for all income groups was 10.95%; for the lowest 20% the expenditure was 15.89%.[10] No surprises there; the poorest always pay more, as a proportion of their income, and they can only buy in small quantities, which is the most expensive way.

Warmth

The website Statista provides a table showing the percentage of weekly expenditure going on clothing in the UK in 2020.[11] This varies according to the income groups between 2.6% and 3.7%, the average for all groups being 3.06%.

Where heating is concerned Ovo energy state that, at the present time, the average cost of heating a home in the UK is £1,042 per year, which works out at 3.5% of average income.[12] Add this to the 3.06% for clothing and we get approximately 6.5% for warmth.

Shelter

Housing costs are usually measured in terms of annual outlay for rental charges or mortgage repayments. Using figures from the Statista website the averages for the period 2011–20 spent in England were: mortgagees 19%, social renters 29%, private renters 36%. Giving an overall average of 28%.[13] The lower figure for social renters is due to the fact that the majority of these are on low incomes, and are more likely to be receiving housing benefits. London, as always, is an exception; Taking private renters alone, the figure for London is 46.4%, more than double that for the rest of England, at 23.1%.

If we take all these figures as indicative, we can see that the relative proportions spent on the three essentials are approximately: food 11%, warmth 6.5% and shelter 28%, giving a total of 45.5 %. This leaves approximately 54.5% that are arguably non-essential. We have to ask ourselves, do these proportions make sense? Do they really reflect what we value? I would suggest that we could pay more for our clothing and food and less for our housing. Let's be honest, clothes are cheap, thanks in large part to the sweatshops of SE Asia. A considerable amount of the clothes found in charity shops are items that have been worn once or twice, then discarded.

According to a *Which* report of November 2019, Britain enjoyed the lowest food prices in the world (after Singapore and the US). In the 31 years between 1988 and 2019 the cost of a typical food shopping basket had reduced by 17%.[14] We waste an enormous amount of food. The food charity FareShare reported that in the UK in 2019 'Over two million tonnes of the food that goes to waste each year is still edible.'[15]

Nobody wants to pay more for anything, but the issue that appears to give all but the highest income groups the most concern is that of housing. Adjectives like 'crazy', 'unbelievable' and 'astronomical' are commonly employed in articles discussing house prices. So perhaps we need to re-assess our priorities on the essentials, not to mention those items in the remaining 54.5%.

With an LVT system in place one could imagine people accepting a trade-off—higher food prices in return for lower house prices and rents—but this would only work domestically. Where farmers producing food for export have to sell in the international food markets, they can only do this with lower prices in order to compete with other countries, whose farm products are also subsidised. So subsidies are likely to continue into the foreseeable future, or until such time as international agreements can be reached, as happens with other trading settlements.

In considering how any land value tax might be applied to the rural situation it is necessary to recognise that the benefits of infrastructure are fewer in rural situations. Areas devoted exclusively to farming do not enjoy the same intensity of infrastructure. Items taken for granted in urban areas—street lighting, mains sewage, bus and train services, gas supplies, broadband etc., are often sparse or non-existent in rural areas.

To help the genuine farmer (as opposed to the 'land manager') there may well be a case for applying a reduced LVT rate to farmland devoted exclusively to food production. This would represent a transfer of the tax burden away from production onto non-productive asset wealth.

In 2009, the Irish Government commissioned a study on the feasibility of introducing a Site Value Tax (SVT), which, in the final proposal, excluded agricultural land altogether.[16] It could be argued that the revenue raised from a tax on marginal agricultural land would be barely worth the administration costs, On the other hand, it would seem reasonable that farmers should pay some charge for the land they use. Unfortunately, the recommendations of the Irish study were not adopted, and Ireland continued with a conventional undifferentiated property tax.

6.3 Unimproved Land Values

The term 'unimproved land value' is widely employed in much writing on LVT, but it can be misleading. What is intended is to make the distinction between a site that has been developed or built upon (improved) and a vacant site where no apparent development has taken place (unimproved). The problem with this term is that it leaves unresolved various anomalies that might arise when trying to establish the actual meaning of 'unimproved' for the purposes of taxation.

Perhaps the commonest example is that of farmland, which from an urban point of view would appear to be unimproved but which may have benefited from generations of careful cultivation, drainage and irrigation. But the evidence of these improvements may not be readily visible and would represent no advantage to any prospective urban developer.

If one were to take unimproved land as meaning, 'in its original natural state', a great deal of farmland would still be covered with dense forest; the familiar quilt of the English countryside that we all love is due to active deforestation, to make way for agriculture that took place centuries ago. At the other extreme are industrial sites, which have been built upon and developed. The necessary improvements in the form of structures, plant and machinery required for the industrial production becomes a liability when the industry goes into decline and the site is abandoned; no little expense is required to clear the site and render it 'unimproved' and usable for some other purpose.

Another example is that of land reclaimed from the sea, which is quite common throughout the world; the so-called unimproved site would still be on the seabed.

I would suggest therefore that the term 'unimproved land value' should be avoided if possible, and only the simple terms 'land value' or 'site value' be used. This would imply the current market value of the site regardless of its history, or whether it is urban or rural.

CHAPTER 7

HOUSING

Buy land, they're not making it anymore.

Mark Twain, American author and humourist

7.1 Winners and Losers

Politicians are always averse to any change in taxation that will create losers who will cost them votes, so they tend to resort to indirect taxes where no obviously disadvantaged group can be identified. Although any change to LVT would create winners and losers, in any part of the economy where land was involved, it is arguably the effect on homeowners that would give politicians most concern.

The losers would be those who hitherto had been the winners over several decades; those who had enjoyed the benefits of increases in their asset wealth completely fortuitously, without any effort on their part. Under LVT this advantage would be arrested and gradually reversed over time, with a reduction of house prices. This would undoubtedly create opposition from those who have got used to the idea of ever-increasing unearned asset wealth and who would not wish to see this advantage eroded. The opposition to LVT would be considerable, not only from these homeowners, but also from the government itself, as Josh Ryan- Collins and co-authors note:

> No government wishes to see the damaging effects of a fall in house prices, especially when almost two-thirds of voters own a property.[1]

The winners would of course be renters and those homeowners who have seen their house values remain static or even go down over the same period, due to being in areas of low or declining land values.

The updating of valuations for any property tax, LVT or otherwise, will always create winners and losers, and the amount of any change, for better or worse, is naturally less where the valuations are frequent. This helps to make the change more acceptable to the losers. The more infrequent the valuations, the greater will be the impact of any change, giving rise to the greater likelihood of protest from the losers. Any updating of the current council tax valuations, neglected for so long, is now viewed with horror by most politicians, knowing full well the impact this would have on the losers in their own constituencies.

And so the situation continues to get worse with each year that passes, and it has now got to the point that any such revaluation would itself require a transition period. Also, those in high-value properties— the wealthy and influential—who would stand to lose the most due to any correction would form a serious opposition, especially where any update was connected to the introduction of LVT.

In Andelson's book *Land Value Taxation Around the World*, Garry Nixon notes that the land-value assessments that operated in Canada in the early part of the 20th century became up to forty years out of date, and whenever attempts were made to correct this situation, 'the landowners (who share a marked disinclination to share their newfound gains), band together and lobby for the status quo.'[2]

As mentioned in Chapter 3, it is generally accepted that the introduction of LVT is more practicable at a local level than at the national level. One of the options in the UK is through reform of the council tax, which I suggest could be done in a way that addresses this issue of winners and losers. (The deficiencies of the present council tax system are described below).

Currently the council tax is based on the capital value of the property (land and building combined), so the first step would have to be a new valuation where building values are separated from site values. From this point, there would be two possibilities, both the same in principle but different in degree: one a change to a full 100% LVT, the other to a partial LVT based on the split-rate system practised successfully in several cities in Pennsylvania, US.

Under the 100% system the new revaluation (which in itself could take a year), would reveal the discrepancies due not only to the new calculations for site values, but also to the consequences of the many years of previous neglect. These discrepancies are likely to be significant, and it would be important to inform all taxpayers in advance of the new dispensation and the estimated future tax liabilities—over a transition period of say 10 years.

Assuming overall revenue neutrality, I would propose that in the first year nothing would change, but taxpayers would be served notice of their current council-tax liability as well as the new liability under LVT—in side-by-side documents. The figures would show the difference between the two levies, divided into ten equal parts, to be added or subtracted as appropriate over the ten-year period, starting in the second year. At the end of the 11th year a full LVT system would be established, and the council-tax calculations could be discontinued. The transition period would avoid any abrupt or disruptive changeover. Those who are to gain from the change would be obliged to defer their gain over the period, and those who are to lose, would have their loss eased over the same period. In this way the winners would be compensating the losers and the figures would be clearly shown in their tax bills every year. It is important that such compensation should be visible, immediate and personalised, and not in the form of some vague promise that other taxes would be reduced in the future.

The second system would be similar in application to the first, except that the ultimate aim would be to arrive at a proportional imposition of the tax divided between the building and the site (say 40/60% or 20/80%), so there would still be some element of tax on the building. This of course is a compromise, but it would make the transition easier, especially for the losers, and would leave open the option of applying a 100% LVT in the future—if it was seen by the taxpayers to be working beneficially. And this is the crucial point. It has to be seen to be working for the majority.

I am inclined to favour this second course as being more practical and more flexible. It is important to get the taxpayers onside, otherwise the whole experiment could founder. Another considerable advantage of adopting this second option is that we in the UK could benefit from the experience of the cities in Pennsylvania, which have practised the split-rate system successfully for many years.[3]

If LVT were to be introduced at the national level, dealing with the issue of winners and losers would be magnified considerably, and a similar formula would need to be devised where the principle of winners compensating losers over a transition period would still apply.

The Council Tax Deficiency:

Local revenue for residential properties is currently collected through the council tax, which a great many commentators report is grossly inefficient and unfair. Apart from the neglect of regular valuations, one serious criticism is with the banding system.

In England, there are eight bands based on what the property would have been valued at in 1991, ranging between the minimum, band A at £40,000, to the maximum, band H at £320,000. Each council is allowed to set its own rates within these bands. In poorer areas the greater number of properties lie in bands A to D, whereas in wealthier areas they tend to be in bands D to H, which means that wealthier areas can raise the same amount of revenue from a lower than normal rate, mainly from high-value properties. This is seen as unfair.

The inequity of the system was summed up in an article by a councillor from Kirklees in West Yorkshire, comparing their situation to that of Westminster:

> About 60% of our homes are in band A... if all their houses are in band H, then they only need to set their tax at a fraction of ours and make the same amount of money.[4]

Within London, in 2019–20, a house in band D in Barking and Dagenham paid a council tax of £1,556, more than double the tax of £752 for a band D house in Westminster.[5] It is often the case that a multimillion-pound band H house in a high-value central location will be paying less council tax than a band D house in a low-value location.

Table 2 shows comparative percentages of the numbers of properties in the tax bands for different cities and counties in England in 2019.

	A %	B %	C %	D %	E %	F %	G %	H %
Leicester	60	19.3	11.6	5	2.5	1	0,4	0.04
Manchester	57	17.3	14.4	6.8	2.4	0.9	0.4	0.04
Leeds	39	21.4	19.2	9.6	6	2.8	2	0.2
Derbyshire	37	22.6	16.7	11	7	3.4	2	0.15
Oxford	4.2	16	31.4	26	11.5	4.6	5.3	1
London	3.9	13.3	27	25	15	7.6	6	1.77
Surrey	2	5.4	18	27	19	12.6	13.5	2.8
Westminster	1.3	5.2	12.6	17.9	18.2	14	18.2	12.5
England	24.3	19.6	22	15.5	9.6	5	3.5	0.6

Table 2 Comparative percentages of the number of properties, in all tax bands, for different English cities and counties, 2019

(Source: Valuation Office Agency, Table CTSOP 1.0, Sept. 2019)

These anomalies arise under the present system where the tax is based on capital values, with an arbitrary cap on maximum payments, disregarding the enormous variations due to location. Were the tax to be based on location values only, these variations would be taken into account, resulting in a higher imposition in the high-value locations. In that sense, the LVT system would be fairer.

The total revenue accruing to the council would amount to whatever was required to meet its commitments, starting from the highest location values and decreasing according to the measure determined by decreasing site values. The council would set the rates within these site-value parameters on a sliding scale rather than a banding system. The bases of the current council tax and a proposed land value tax are very different. Within the constraints of the planning laws, a land value tax is not concerned with what is on the site, but only with a payment for the use of it.

7.2 Getting on the Property Ladder

This expression arose from the time when ordinary homeowners realised that their home had value not only as somewhere to live but also as an investment. It became evident that, over the long term, increasing house values provided a better return on capital than savings accounts. Also, paying rent to a landlord when you could be paying off a mortgage did not make sense to most people. The mortgage lenders were eager to oblige, and with the demutualisation of building societies in the 1980s the banks were more involved.

Lending grew enormously, became overextended, and led eventually to the financial collapse of 2007–08.

It was all based on the hope that house prices would go on rising forever, and everyone wanted to be a beneficiary. But the rising house prices were caused by an increasing demand for a scarce commodity—in the right locations; in the wrong locations prices barely moved. In either case there was no increase of real wealth. Josh Ryan-Collins et al. describe the events of this period of rapid mortgage lending as the financialisation of land.[6]

The figures of Table 3 have been compiled from data on the Design Laboratory website, which gives comparative values of average annual wages, cars and houses from 1900 to 2019. Section A shows the actual values, section B the equivalent 2019 values, adjusted for inflation.

As can be seen, prior to World War Two adjusted house prices had risen and fallen more or less in equal measure; by 1940 the price of a house was only 9% more than in 1900. After World War Two house prices rose sharply, then stabilised for a period in the 1950s, before beginning the inexorable rise that would continue to the present time. Homeowners recognised that in the longer term their home would generally appreciate in value despite temporary declines during economic recessions.

Of course, property developers had always understood the opportunities available in appreciating property values and also that land values varied according to the demand for good locations. Their

Year	A Actual values (£)			2019 £10 equiv	B Adjusted values (£)			Wage/ house ratio
	Wage	Car	House		Wage	Car	House	
1900	58	200	200	1219	7069	24377	26815	3.79
1910	62	220	330	1168	7242	25698	38547	5.32
1920	186	270	320	443	8244	11967	14183	1.72
1930	131	295	450	648	8491	19121	29169	3.43
1940	181	310	530	555	10048	17209	29422	2.93
1950	332	600	1829	339	11281	20388	62152	5.51
1960	634	800	2385	228	14480	18271	54470	3.76
1970	1204	1090	4690	153	18470	16721	71946	3.89
1980	5069	3550	22246	42	21556	15096	94600	4.39
1990	11820	9000	56365	22	26643	20286	127048	4.77
2000	18848	12780	83333	17	31461	21332	139101	4.42
2010	25882	17120	163052	13	32910	21769	206057	6.26
2019	30420	19995	235298	10	30420	19995	235298	7.73

Table 3 UK average values of annual wages, cars and houses, 1900– 2019

(Source: The Design Laboratory ttp://thedesignlab.co.uk/costofliving2015/ukupdate.php?uid=36)

success depended on their ability to make advantageous choices about where and when to buy and invest and when to sell. From 1960 onwards, their ranks were swollen by a growing number of aspiring homeowners who saw the same opportunities. This is when the idea of getting on the property ladder became current.

Figure 14 shows three different types of tenure: homeownership, private renting and social renting, in the period from 1918 to 2014.

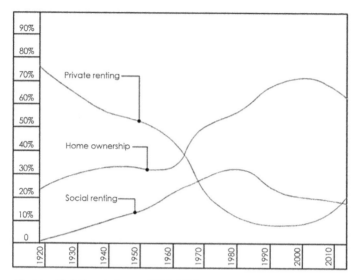

Fig.14   Variations in tenure, 1918–2014
(Source: ONS, webarchive, National Archives)

As can be seen, with homeownership there is a sudden increase from the 1960s onwards, peaking around the year 2000. From 1918 onwards private renting declined until reaching a low point in the 1990s, and then starting to rise again. It's notable that these two graph lines almost mirror each other. Social renting reached a peak in the early 1980s and has been in decline ever since

It has to be borne in mind that during the period in question tenure varied considerably. In the early years the majority of people were private renters; social renting was only just becoming established, but it increased constantly after World War One, until reaching a peak in the 1980s. The trends shown could also be seen to represent the changes of influence on politicians exercised by the different social blocs through the vote.

From the middle of the period, the politicians would have been more concerned with the votes to be gained from the growing number of social renters, up until the 1980s. After that their concern turned towards the interests of homeowners. In the case of homeowners (those safely on the property ladder), there was, and still is, a vested interest in constantly increasing house prices. This increase is not due to any increase in the overall wealth of the community, but merely an increase of existing asset value for the homeowners. The media, encouraged by many politicians and economists, still see any such increase as a matter for celebration. LVT would of course arrest this process and gradually reverse it, so it is likely to be opposed by the many homeowners who would see themselves as the losers in any such radical change.

The graphs of Figure 15 show comparative costs of cars and houses in relation to average wages, for the period 1900 to 2020. They are based on the figures shown in Table 3B. (The use of adjusted values are more meaningful, especially in the earlier years).

In 1900 a house cost just under four times the annual wage, a car 3.4 times; a car was certainly a luxury. Wages rose slowly from 1900 to 1935, then more rapidly, reaching a maximum about 2008, Car prices fluctuated in the earlier decades, but stabilised after about 1952. Car prices and annual wages were about the same in 1968, after which car prices were always lower.

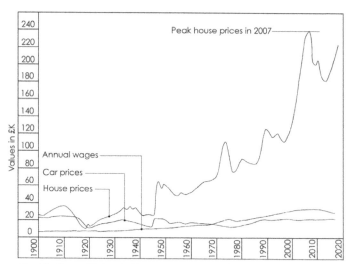

Fig.15 Cost of living indicators: Average values in £ (adjusted) for
Houses, Cars and Annual Wages, 1900–2016

At the end of World War Two, house prices jumped
from £26,536 in 1945 to £66,700 in 1947, before
returning to £50,421 in 1954. Thereafter house prices
continued to climb—with peaks in the 1970s and
1990s—until reaching another peak in 2007, just
before the economic crash of 2008. The ratio for
average wages to house prices fluctuated in the first
50 years no doubt due to distortions caused by the two
wars and the 1930s depression, but the ratio in 1970
(3.89) had returned almost to what it had been in 1900
(3.79). Thereafter the ratio increased steadily until
it had reached 7.26 in 2007 and 7.73 in 2019. For the
younger generation, buying a home from their own
resources was becoming impossible.

Private renting, which had previously been in decline,
started to increase again in the 1990s. The annual

minimum wage in 2019 was about £16,000, well over double the average wage in 1900, but taxes on the individual then were less onerous than in 2019. However, due to the lack of social and welfare provisions in 1900, there was a larger proportion of the working population that could be considered 'poor'.

7.3 Affordable Housing

As with any commodity, it is the combination of the price demanded and the financial means of the prospective buyer that renders it affordable or not. Housing is no different. House prices have been rising inexorably at least since the 1960s and continue to do so, especially in the most sought-after areas, such as London and the South East. However, since the economic collapse of 2007–08 these increases have not been matched by any commensurate increase of wages and salaries above the general level of inflation. Even in the less sought-after areas of the country, where the increases have been less marked, people still have to struggle to find the down payment for a mortgage. This situation is nothing new, but it has become far more acute in recent years. The consequence is that, since 2000, home ownership has been in decline and private renting has been increasing—as shown in Figure 14.

The problem of housing affordability has been around at least since the end of World War One, when the Homes for Heroes programme was established, leading later to subsidised council housing which, although a form of welfare, was an effective solution to the problem of affordability for many years. The council-housing stock thereafter was added to with greater or lesser enthusiasm by all governments until being set into reverse by the 'sell-off' policy of the Thatcher government in the 1980s. This policy of course added to the number of homeowners who then had a vested interest in continually rising house prices, not to mention a new group of grateful Tory voters. But council housing, rightly or wrongly, has always carried a stigma; given the choice and the financial means, the majority of people would choose to live in the leafy suburbs rather than the council estate. And the crucial phrase here is financial means; without the financial means, many things become unaffordable, including housing.

At the present time, amongst economists and commentators on housing, various reasons are suggested for high house prices:

- Low housing supply
- Low interest rates, and therefore cheap mortgages
- The attraction, to investors, of an appreciating asset
- Government policies encouraging home ownership

No doubt all of these factors, either singly or in combination, have an effect on causing house prices to rise, but the one thing that is rarely mentioned is the land-value factor, which is the indicator of the demand for houses. In the most sought-after locations, it is the ownership of the location—rather than the ownership of the house—that provides the best return, which accrues through the economic rent, either directly at the time of sale or indirectly—as explained in Chapter 8. It is worth considering each of the above factors individually.

Low Housing Supply

The solution to the problem of housing supply offered by politicians (and many economic advisors) is simply to build more houses hoping that, by the law of supply and demand, the increase of supply will bring prices down. But they do not recognise that the price of a house is related not only to the value of the building, but also the value of the site upon which it stands. In high-value areas the site value may be as much as four times that of the building value, so any increase of house building can only affect 20% of the total price; the 80% due to site value will continue to rise regardless. Land does not obey the law of supply and demand, because the supply of land is fixed.

This last statement has to be qualified: Although no more land can be created, sites can always be supplied for particular purposes through a change of use or simply through demolition and re-use. But these changes of use are rare, and in any case controlled through the planning system.[7] Since the 1980s, a substantial amount of public land has been sold to the private sector for commercial development, including housing.[8] So there is a supply, but the competition is intense for such sites, and once acquired, the release for development is strictly controlled to the best advantage of the landholder (see 7.4 below, Land Banking).

A further point on this allocation of value between the house and the site is one relating to actual wealth. Houses represent real wealth, land does not (see Chapter 13, Definitions). So, in the example given above, only 20% of the total value is due to real wealth, the remaining 80% is a paper asset, a value that is not based on any tangible asset or productive increase. As Ryan-Collins et al. note, 'When the value of land under a house goes up, the total productive capacity of the economy is unchanged.'[9]

Housebuilders and developers have a built-in aversion to providing affordable housing; they make the bulk of their profits from building and selling high-priced properties. They will go to any lengths to wriggle out of the section 106 requirements for affordable housing that are a condition imposed by local councils for the granting of planning permission.

In 2012, the housebuilders and other property interests strongly influenced the drawing up of the government's National Planning Policy Framework (NPPF), which included a 'viability assessment' clause. This clause made it easier for the housebuilders and developers to negotiate their way out of the section 106 requirements by arguing that if the conditions were too onerous the scheme would become 'unviable'. This was simply another way of saying that their profits would be reduced. In his book *The Property Lobby*, Bob Colenutt describes all this in considerable detail.[10]

Ireland suffers the same problem with housing as England. Conall Boyle, former lecturer in economics and statistics at Birmingham City University, wrote an interesting article showing that the increase of house building in Ireland between 1975 and 2015 did not help to bring prices down.[11]

It is the site-value factor that has the greatest effect on house prices in high-value urban areas and the ever-rising prices are exacerbated through land hoarding and land speculation, creating an artificial shortage. The consequent increase in prices is always to the benefit of the landholders, whose ranks are now increased by the new homeowners.

Low Interest Rates

An article of February 2020 for the University College London IIPP blog by Josh Ryan-Collins is entitled 'When it comes to high house prices, it's not enough to just blame low interest rates'[12] Also in his book *Why You Can't Afford a Home*, he notes that, 'However fast you can build, banks can create new credit faster.'[13]

Low interest rates mean cheaper borrowing, which includes mortgage lending. Whenever a bank lends, it is creating credit for the borrower, and the amount credited is effectively new money. Certainly, greater access to mortgages results in many more prospective buyers looking for houses, which inevitably raises prices, especially in the best locations. There is general agreement that the economic collapse of 2007–08 originated in the US and was brought on by the irresponsible granting of mortgage credit to so-called sub-prime borrowers. But the same practices were being carried out in the UK and worldwide. In another article, Ryan-Collins suggests that this situation was more the result of deregulation and entry of the banks into the mortgage industry than by low interest rates. He notes that 'interest rates were not particularly low in the 1980s.'[14] So although low interest rates are an encouragement to borrowing, there is some doubt that they are the prime cause of high house prices (see Box 1, below, for a brief history of UK interest rates).

Prior to deregulation, for most people, mortgages were only obtainable through building societies, which were not allowed to lend more than they had from savers' deposits. The commercial banks, on the other hand, operated under the system of fractional-reserve banking whereby they could lend far more than their reserves. Mortgage loans, in consequence, became more readily accessible, leading eventually to irresponsible lending and the financial crash of 2008.

Attraction to Investors of an Appreciating Asset

This is a more likely cause. As noted in item 7.2, above, the attraction of housing as a financial asset became more evident in the 1980s and 1990s, not only to professional investors, but also to ordinary homeowners. Both saw it as an excellent way of increasing their wealth and security, if they were able to buy into an area with good growth prospects. Of course, in the most sought-after areas, the homeowners were competing not only with professional investors but also wealthy foreign buyers who bid prices up to extraordinary levels, especially in the capital.

The great attraction of housing to investors is that, over the long term, it is invariably an appreciating asset (see Figure 15). The house, as with any physical commodity, depreciates in value over time, but the land on which it stands can only appreciate with the demand. Where, as in the example above, the site value is 80% of the total, the appreciating portion—the site value—far outweighs that which is depreciating—the house value. Even in low-value areas, where the proportions may be reversed, but where the house is well maintained and depreciation slight, there may still be an investment interest, however slowly the site value may be increasing.

Government Policies

From the 1980s onwards, governments have pursued policies to encourage home ownership, which could be seen as subsidies for existing and prospective homeowners. The 'Right to Buy' policy for council tenants, introduced in the 1980s, is well known, but there was also MIRAS (mortgage interest relief at source), which encouraged mortgage borrowing, and which lasted from 1983 to 2000. Since then, there have been a number of schemes designed in different ways to enable homeownership or stimulate housing supply, such as 'Help to Buy', 'Rent to Buy' and 'Build to Rent'. These schemes are well described in an article by Christopher Walker, a housing specialist and government advisor.[15] The exemption of capital gains tax on first homes could also be seen as an encouragement to homeownership. All of these schemes in different ways encourage prospective buyers to enter the market, which inevitably has the effect of raising prices.

The best solution to all of these problems would be to introduce a land value tax, which would arrest the rise of the land-value factor, keep prices under control and make land banking and speculation unprofitable. Only then will housing become affordable.

Box 1. <u>UK Interest Rates</u>

Private banks are able to charge whatever interest rates they wish, but normally these are closely related to the interest rate they in turn have to pay for borrowing from the Bank of England. So, effectively, interest rates are determined by the Bank of England—which was established in 1694. The history of the rate shows distinct periods of stability and other periods of volatility.

For the first 25 years the rate varied between 6% and 3% then, in 1719, stabilised at 5%. This rate remained constant for the next 103 years until 1822, then for 23 years varied between 2.5% and 6%. In 1840 the rate entered a long period of volatility that lasted till 1932, during which time it varied between 2% and 10%. Another period of stability, for 19 years, from 1932 to 1951, maintained a rate of 2%, except for a brief blip to 4% in 1939 at the start of World War Two. From 1951 a second period of volatility that lasted until 2009 saw the rate vary between 2% and 17%. In 2009 the rate dropped to the unprecedented level of 0.5% and has been at or near this level ever since.[16]

7.4 Land Banking

Land banking, also known as land hoarding, is nothing new but has become a more noticeable issue in recent years due to the increasing housing problem, which is seen as largely a matter of supply. House builders complain of the lack of access to, or the excessive cost of building sites, as the main reason for their inability to deliver the houses required. The theory is that building is restricted by the high cost of land acquisition—which is reflected in the final price, hence the high house prices.

The housebuilders are also inclined to blame the restrictive planning laws (which constrain the release of greenbelt land for development) and they constantly press for their relaxation. They disregard the fact that there is a large amount of brownfield land that is capable of redevelopment.[17] The developers and housebuilders naturally prefer the easiest route—the development of clear uncontaminated land. This is preferable to the messy business of decontamination and clearance involved with brownfield land, whose potential future value is uncertain.

The temptation to hoard land, whose increase in value is assured, and where there is no incentive to develop, is described in Brett Christopher's book *The New Enclosure*, where he speaks of 'developers consciously, strategically deciding to bank land rather than build on it.'[18]

A great deal of course depends on the granting of planning permissions, which for a former greenbelt site can increase the value by as much as 275 times.[19] By comparison, the increase on brownfield would be a great deal less, as it would involve remediation work and would be a much longer-term investment. So, for developers, the release of greenbelt land is the main prize. The existing landowner is well aware of this and aims to exact his share from the future uplift of value.

On the anticipation of permission being granted, the claims to this uplift are already being made by many interested parties, except, ironically, those to whom this uplift truly belongs, the general public. Also, the transactions of these claims may take place several times over before, or even if, a single brick is laid.

It is quite possible for a developer to gain planning permission for a site on the strength of a detailed project submission, which he hasn't the slightest intention of building. Once the permission is obtained (and the increased value established) the developer can sell the project on 'with planning permission' to another developer, who is obliged to carry out the scheme within three years. Even if this time limit is allowed to lapse, any future buyer knows that the site has previously been granted permission, and this makes all the difference to the potential value. This is an example of the collection of the economic rent in advance (see Chapter 8, Rent Collected in Advance). All these are paper exercises, but at each stage money is made by the seller, and whoever finally owns the site is often content to sit tight in the knowledge that its value will continue to increase. The logical outcome is the accumulation of valuable sites with planning permission, actual or potential.

Housebuilders and developers acquire sites in this way and have no real incentive to build on them as their value is appreciating in any case, without effort. They release sites into the market deliberately slowly to keep the prices high. They have to do this to maintain a profit, after all the previous claimants have taken theirs in advance.

This ongoing scandal is described very well by Oliver Wainwright, a journalist and architectural commentator. In a Guardian article he revealed that, in 2015 the UK's biggest housebuilders were sitting on 600,000 plots of land that had planning permission.[20] In another article, the planning manager of the Council for the Protection of Rural England, Paul Miner, said that developers maintain their profitability by 'drip-feeding homes onto the market at a pace that best suits their profits.'[21] Christophers also discusses at length the consequences of land privatisation, the selling off of public land that began in earnest with the neoliberal policies of the Thatcher administration in the 1980s. The policy was ideologically based on the belief that land was always more efficiently used under private ownership—a dubious claim. He goes on to show that the three main consequences of land privatisation have been 'increased land banking', a shift towards a 'rentier economy' and widespread 'social dislocation.'[22]

An experiment in dealing with land banking has been taking place in Ireland with the Vacant-Site Levy that came into force in 2017. But so far it has proved difficult to enforce and easy to avoid; the resulting revenue being a fraction of what had been anticipated. The scheme appears to have been a failure; many people agree with the idea in principle but the drafting and administration has apparently been insufficiently rigorous.[23]

Land speculators have been around a long time—as noted in the early settlement of North America in Chapter 2. The situation mentioned above is merely a variation on this old technique; now exacerbated by the peculiarities of the planning system. The acquisition of a planning consent is clearly a very valuable and saleable asset, and a number of individuals and organisations are able to privately profit from the system.

The Labour administrations after the World War Two were very much aware of this 'betterment' and attempted to curtail the resultant profiteering, but without success. (see Chapter 4, 20th Century History). To make matters worse, the Conservatives, who regained power in 1959 introduced a provision— section 5 in the 1961 Land Compensation Act—which allowed landowners to add the future betterment value, the 'hope value', into their selling price, a virtual speculator's charter. This provision is the main cause of the high cost of building land at the outset, which, after each player adds on their own profit, results in the final high cost of housing. The provision should be one of the first things to be repealed in any move towards land reform. There is now an increasing view among many politicians, that it should be abolished, or at.least amended.[24]

CHAPTER 8

OTHER ECONOMIC RENT
COLLECTION PRACTICES

For how long does an evil have to be
practiced for it to become a good?

Andrew MacLaren (1883–1975): Independent
Labour MP for Burslem (1922–45)

8.1 Economic Rent Collected in Advance

As mentioned in the basic principles of Chapter 1, the
economic rent of land arises inexorably and is collected
by whoever is in control of the land, whether an
individual or a government. This economic rent varies
according to the productivity on each site and is known
by economists as a 'differential rent'. The differential
economic rent was identified at the beginning of the
19th century by the political economist David Ricardo
(see Chapter 13, Definitions). In Ricardo's time, theories
were based on an agrarian economy, where fertility was
the principal factor in determining both productivity
and the corresponding land value. In later years, with
the growth of cities, productivity became more related
to location within an agglomeration, but the principle

of the economic rent still applied, and differentials became even more pronounced.

Whether in an agrarian or an urban situation, for a given amount of input, there is always a difference in productivity for any site in relation to the marginal or least productive site. This difference, or surplus, determines the amount any landlord can extract from the tenant for the use of the site. This extractable rent may be seen as the surplus that remains when all other costs of production have been met. What is seldom appreciated is that this surplus may be anticipated and collected in advance by speculators, who understand the causes that increase land values.

In the early days in Britain, entitlement to the surplus was decided either by force of arms or the general acceptance that the monarch held total control and was therefore entitled through ownership to any surplus wealth. In later years the monarch was obliged to share this entitlement with a growing nobility who exercised control over their own domains, and collected the economic surplus from the peasants, farmers, artisans and traders, who were the real wealth creators. This was a manifestation of the 'rentier' system in England that still operates to this day (see Chapter 13, Definitions).

Traditionally, with this system, the surplus was collected in arrears after the wealth had been created. The landowners would simply take a proportion of whatever was produced for their own use and pass on an agreed amount to the monarch. This represented the collection of the economic surplus—the economic rent—within an agrarian economy.

The collection of the economic rent in advance began with land speculation during the enclosures, but especially during the industrial revolution, in the transformation from a rural to an urban economy. As villages and towns grew into cities, urban land became ever more valuable, and the corresponding rents obtainable through ownership of such land became more profitable. The acquisition of tracts of land in anticipation of this growth gave rise to widespread speculation. The new owner may have developed the land in his own interest, but in many cases the land was simply held out of use until surrounding values rose, then sold off in small parcels at a profit.

This is how the economic rent was collected in advance. No investment was made, no work was done on the land in question, the speculator simply waited whilst his asset wealth increased from the activity of the surrounding community. He then collected his gain, when the time suited him even before any economic activity towards wealth creation on the land had begun. The collection of the economic rent in advance is a very lucrative and risk-free means of gaining wealth. Two contemporary examples of this are worth noting:

In London, in the 1990s, the Jubilee Line extension had the effect of raising site values surrounding the new stations. The beneficiaries of this increase were the landlords and property owners occupying these sites, who were able to raise their rents or sell their properties for a considerable profit, even before the work on the project was complete. It is recorded that the revenue derived from the overall increased land values could have easily paid for the construction of the project, which was financed by taxpayers, not only in London, but throughout the country.[1]

Also in London, the Crossrail project has, since its inception in 2008, given rise to a significant increase in house prices and commercial property rents near the proposed stations. Reports by several organisations show increases in residential values of up to 83% in certain locations.[2] A *Guardian* article of August 2018, noted that the total uplift in property values could be as much as £20 billion by 2026—'all being siphoned into the pockets of private landowners.'[3] The project is expected to open sometime in 2022, but long before that event large windfall profits will have already accrued to existing property owners or to those who have bought into the right locations in anticipation of future increases. These profits can be realised at any time even before a single train has started to run.

Thus, the return on the investment, in the form of economic rent, may be collected in advance by others who have contributed nothing to the financing or construction of the project. To those who have made a good profit and moved on, it doesn't matter if the scheme never opens.

A further means of advanced collection has already been mentioned in the previous chapter under Land Banking, where I describe the selling on of projects 'with planning permission'. At each transaction a profit is made, which is due to the value of the consent attached to the site. The gain to the seller is collected in advance of any actual development that might (or might not) take place.

8.2 Collection Through Rent Absorption

Any increase of productivity within an enterprise, for whatever reason, will naturally accrue to the ultimate controller or beneficial owner. Landowners are amongst those who will absorb any surplus of profitability by increasing the rents chargeable. Thus, no advantage will be gained for those lower down the hierarchy of production, even though they may have been instrumental in bringing about the increase in the first place. This phenomenon is mentioned by Josh Ryan-Collins et al:

> As the economy grows, landowners can increase the rent they charge non-owners, to absorb all the additional value that their tenants (such as workers, shopkeepers and industrialists) generate.[4]

This is a case of the creaming-off by owners of any surplus arising within the ranks of the non-owners, which may be seen as rent absorption. This is a time-honoured activity. Another type of rent absorption is due not to any increase in production but simply to government benevolence in the form of tax relief or welfare payments. A good example of this was described by Churchill in his book *The People's Rights*, where he records the lifting of the penny-a-day toll on Waterloo bridge in 1878. Although the intention was the relief of this burden on the workers obliged to cross the bridge each day, the actual effect was the increase of rents by sixpence a week on the south side of the river where the workers lived.[5] Another example is given in Duncan Pickard's book *The Lie of the Land* in which he describes the consequences of farmland being de-rated in the 1930s:

Many tenant farmers had their rents increased to offset the removal of the liability to pay rates.[6]

These are both examples of the unintended consequences of legislation designed for the relief of certain groups that resulted only in maintaining the income source for the landlords. A more up to date example of such misdirected welfare is with the government's current system of housing benefit for low earners. Instead of actually helping the low earners, all the system does is maintain the high rental charges for the landlord. Instead of subsidising landlords in this way, an LVT would actually reduce the rents and therefore help the low earners directly. The landlords, or any other rent-seekers, will always see an opportunity for taking up the slack. They are not concerned with the cause of any increased rental possibility, but only with the best means for exploiting it when it arises.

CHAPTER 9

OBJECTIONS AND OBSTACLES

Only the little people pay taxes.

Leona Helmsley (1920-2007):
Billionaire American businesswoman

9.1 Typical Objections to LVT

These are some of the routine objections raised by opponents of LVT:

- LVT is a form of wealth confiscation
- The 'Poor-Widow' objection
- Separate valuation of land would be too difficult.

The following are my responses.

LVT is a Form of Wealth Confiscation

In the Mirrlees Review of 2011, the comment is made that there are those who see the taxation of wealth 'as the unjustified confiscation of private property'[1] —a view that is more likely to be held by the wealthy than the less wealthy. To respond to this charge we have to return to the principle of 'ability to pay', noted in

Chapter 1, and the issue of 'identification and measurement', discussed in the Introduction.

LVT is generally considered to be a wealth tax (or one might say a tax on the ownership of the access to wealth). It is also an excellent way of identifying the location of that wealth and providing a means of measuring it.

No one is trying to disguise the fact that LVT would shift the burden of taxation off the less wealthy onto the more wealthy; indeed this is one of its main purposes. For many years politicians of all colours have seen themselves as champions of the poor. They spend endless time and effort devising legislation to improve the condition of the poor by trying to reduce the inequalities of wealth distribution that exist within society. These efforts have been going on for decades in vain, for they deal only with symptoms and never face up to the causes. One of the prime causes of the maldistribution of wealth is due to the misunderstanding and misuse of the economic rent of land. LVT faces up to this problem directly and head-on.

As mentioned in Chapter 7, with any change toward a system of LVT there would be winners and losers. The losers would be the wealthy who for generations have reaped the unearned benefit of the economic rent at the expense of the rest of society. With some honourable exceptions, they will no doubt cry 'foul', 'confiscation', 'class envy', 'Communism' and whatever else they can think of to protect their privilege. What would be confiscated is the capacity of private landowners and speculators to increase their unearned wealth gained from the work of others, and thereby exacerbating the ever-widening wealth gap.

The acceptance of LVT amongst ordinary citizens would depend on their acceptance of the principle of just deserts and not on exploiting some opportunity to gain something for nothing. I suggest that the winners would include everyone—even the rich. The necessary openness of an LVT system would increase efficiency at all levels of production. The owners of industries and service organisations would benefit by being able to sell their products and services more readily to a wealthier population. In 1914, in order to solve the problem of employee turnover, Henry Ford doubled the pay of his workers, resulting in a significant increase in his company's production and profits.[2]

Companies could also save money otherwise spent on paying expensive lawyers and accountants to devise clever ways of avoiding taxes; a waste of talent that could otherwise be employed for a more socially beneficial purpose.

A common theme that recurs frequently with objectors is the one of fairness: that taxing wealth in the form of accumulated assets is unfair. It may be acceptable to tax any income derived from an asset, such as that from renting out a house, or interest on shares or savings, but not in order to 'confiscate' a portion of the capital value of the asset itself, which is how the effect of LVT is often seen.

The response to this objection depends on the acceptance of the three classical divisions of economic reward: wages to labour, rent to land and interest to capital. Unfortunately, the neoclassical/neoliberal view that still dominates economic thinking at the present time does not recognise land as being different from any other capital asset, so a tax on it is more likely to be seen as confiscation. And so it is basically a matter of education or, where the neoclassical view is concerned, re-education.

Any acceptance of LVT in principle amongst economists will require a basic change in this attitude—towards the status of land. The issue of fairness is directly related to the perennial objection concerning the ability to pay, proffered curiously by the rich as well as the poor. This argues that simply having a valuable asset does not mean one is able to pay some new tax, at least not without having to sell or mortgage the asset. There is some truth in this, but it disregards the fact that LVT would be a replacement for other taxes (see Chapter 10, Taxes to Eliminate, Modify or Keep) and also that there would need to be a gradual transition period (see Chapter 7, Winners and Losers). Undoubtedly, a tax on land would adversely affect those whose wealth was invested in land assets, but only in the sense of surrendering a proportion of the increase in value created in any case by the community at large.

On reading through many objections, one gets the sense that the objectors are making the erroneous assumptions that LVT would be an additional tax that would be introduced overnight, which would of course be highly disruptive. Were these misconceptions to be corrected, the strength of the objections would be much reduced. The issue of the ability to pay is one of principle—determining who should pay and how much.

This takes us back to the basic principles behind all taxation, discussed in Chapter 1. As has been said earlier, all taxes have to come from some form of wealth or wealth-creation activity. To describe such taxes as confiscatory is nonsense. It would be more helpful to see taxes as contributions, towards enabling a society to function as it should.

The 'Poor Widow' Objection

The poor widow objection has been around for at least a hundred years; at least since Winston Churchill expressed his exasperation in a speech to parliament in 1909.[3] It has become a shibboleth that is instantly brandished, even by those who admit to having only a vague knowledge of LVT; by some uncanny means they seem to know all about the poor widow. In more recent times it is expressed as the problem of the 'asset-rich, income-poor', or more specifically, elderly people having only a state pension but still living in the large family home—especially widows in mansions. This issue has been discussed to exhaustion, and it is largely agreed amongst LVT advocates that the best solution is the deferment system, whereby any tax increase arising from a change to LVT is deferred and settled out of the estate at death, or from the proceeds at any prior point of sale.[4]

The poor widow objection is based on certain assumptions that in any case may not be true, namely that:

- With LVT the tax liability will always go up rather than down.

- The house in which the poor widow lives is in a high-value location.
- Any revaluation assessing land and buildings separately will be to the detriment of those living in large houses.

It tends to be forgotten that the poor widow is already paying a council tax based on selling price values. If she is in a large house, it is likely to fall within the current highest band H already, which she is having to pay out of her pension now. If the house is in a low-value or even average-value area, under LVT her tax bill might go down. It should be remembered that within the current valuations, or any new revaluation, it is only relative values that matter, not absolute values; the total tax take is the same. Since the last valuation in 1991, relative land values may have changed a great deal, but this is much less likely with relative building values. If there is any change in fortune for the poor widow, it will relate more to where she is living than the size of her house; it is quite possible that she could gain rather than lose.

Valuing Land Separately Would Be Too Difficult

This must be one of the weakest of objections, and it seems to be peculiar to Britain. Other countries that have practiced LVT or have some form of LVT in place report no particular problems with making separate valuations for land and buildings. The Danes had a National LVT from 1957 to 1960, during which time the Danish economy prospered.[5] They have had local LVT since 1926 with revaluations every four years.

Since 1998, valuations have been updated annually.[6] The Australians have for many years employed different forms of LVT in different states, with regular revaluations, and do not report any special difficulties. Many towns in the USA practice the 'split-rate' system, which requires separate valuations for land and buildings on a regular basis.

In 1964 a land value survey was carried out in the town of Whitstable in Kent for the Rating and Valuation Association. The valuer's report included valuation lists and site value maps and was carried out without any insuperable problems. In his conclusion the valuer commented that, 'the field work involved in valuing site only is very much less than valuing site plus improvements.'[7] In a follow up survey done in 1973, the same valuer said, 'The field work was done with notable speed.'

In a 2010 report for The Green Party of Scotland, the environmental scientist Andy Wightman commented:

Valuers in Scotland have no difficulty in general in valuing land and property for a range of purposes.[8]

With reference to a land value survey carried out for the Inland Revenue in 1910, he also commented:

If the Edwardians can manage to survey the ownership and management of all land in Britain and Ireland with paper and ink, there is no reason why modern aerial imagery, computerised mapping and GIS technology cannot do the same a hundred years later.

In 2005, a land value tax study was also carried out for Oxfordshire County Council.[9] The study group included a qualified surveyor who reported, 'Valuations based on the undeveloped value of land present no special problems for a professional valuer.'

Professional valuers no doubt have their own sophisticated methods for making separate site valuations, but for the layman there is a simple method known as the residual system, which is easy to understand: If you take the overall value of the property (the selling price), and deduct the replacement cost of the building, allowing for age depreciation, the remainder would be the site value. Insurance companies are continuously engaged in assessing the replacement costs of buildings for insurance purposes. For a newly built house, the process would be even easier: where one would simply deduct the builder's costs and profit without any depreciation.

Another possibility for valuing the land without contestation from the landholder is through the method of self-valuation. This allows the landholder to make his own assessment of the value, with the condition that the taxing authority reserves the right to purchase the land at the declared price. O'Regan notes that in New Zealand this method was incorporated in the general property tax of 1879.[10]

The Land Registry

A further reason that is often raised by opponents of LVT, for the supposed difficulty of making a comprehensive valuation, is the fact that the Land Registry is only 85% complete. This is largely due to the difficulty of tracing landowners who do not wish to reveal their identity, who hide behind offshore shell companies, or obscure agencies. After the government proposed the privatisation of the Land Registry in 2014, it was discovered that all the potential bidders had links to offshore tax havens.[11] The proposed legislation was subsequently withdrawn.

Although it is obviously preferable for the Registry to be complete, it is not absolutely essential. Assuming that the current occupant of the site is, for whatever reason, not able to reveal the identity of the owner, then the LVT charge would be served on the occupant who would then be able to deduct the same amount from whatever rent he or she was paying to the agent. Where vacant sites with no occupant were concerned, the government could, via the international media, declare its intention to expropriate the site, unless the owner came forward within six months.

General Notes:

- Objections to LVT are dealt with comprehensively in Mark Wadsworth's blog: http://kaalvtn. blogspot.fr/p/index.html
- Also refer to the FAQs of Land Value Taxation Campaign's site: http://www.landvaluetax.org/ frequently-asked-questions/
- Further useful comment on the subject of valuations can be found in the paper by Dr Tony Vickers, 'Questions around the Smart Tax', on the ALTER website:
  http://libdemsalter.org.uk/en/article/2013/737148/ questions-and- answers-on-lvt-a-need-to-update-them

9.2 Obstacles to Implementing LVT

There would be several formidable obstacles to the adoption of LVT.

- Resistance from landowners and speculators
- General resistance to 'wealth taxes'
- Lack of understanding of the principles of LVT
- Political resistance
- Academic resistance

Resistance From Landowners and Speculators

It is understandable that landowners would resist any system that would reduce the benefits they derive from the collection of the economic rent. LVT would of course divert this collection away from landowners and towards the public purse.

Historically landowners have always held great power and influence over politicians and within established institutions. Indeed, they have themselves often been the politicians or leading figures within these institutions, and so there is a built-in vested interest against any form of land reform that would alter the status quo—the 'rentier' system of land ownership that has underwritten the wealth of the rich over many centuries.

In his book, *Why We Can't Afford the Rich*, Andrew Sayer says, 'The infiltration and capture of the state by the rich has been a piecemeal process, with roots going back decades.'[12] Also, Collier comments: 'Vested interests know far more about the nature of their advantage than public officials can possibly know.'[13]

Whereas the landowner may be seen as a passive actor in this scenario, the land speculator is actively engaged in trading in land; buying when the price is low and selling when the value has risen. Profits accrue due to surrounding development and increased demand for new sites; a demand which he has not necessarily had any hand in creating. Rather than the landlord's regular collection of the economic rent over the long term, the speculator is more interested in the immediate profit to be made by the sale of a site whose value has been enhanced by adjacent development or publicly funded infrastructure. The speculator will deliberately hold the site out of use in order to bid up the value.

Land speculation of this kind has always been viewed with disapproval, as adding nothing to the public benefit, but as simply a means of personal enrichment, without any contribution to society. Certainly, a speculator may make a misjudgement and find that the anticipated development does not take place, but he would still probably be able to sell off the land for almost what he paid for it.

Property developers who buy sites and develop them through actual building work are serving a useful social purpose, but they are also very aware that in a growing community it is the site-value factor that will enable them to command a good price for their development. In a developing community, time is always on the side of the land speculator. So it is clear that in a developing community, land ownership, in whatever form it might take, can provide considerable unearned financial advantage. This advantage would be threatened by the onset of LVT and would not be surrendered easily.

After the publication of Henry George's *Progress and Poverty* in 1879, the idea of LVT became very popular throughout the world and reached its heyday just prior to World War One, but the landowning interests were able to marshal the forces necessary to organise an effective resistance, politically, academically and philosophically.

Walter Rybeck provides a historical example of the landlord's and banker's resistance to LVT, in the case of the 1917 Wright Act in California, related to the funding of an irrigation scheme. The Act stipulated that the finance should be raised only from a tax on the land-value increases due to the scheme. Rybeck notes that:

> Big landlords, bankers and private utilities fought mercilessly in the courts to undermine the Wright Act.[14]

In this event the landowners lost the case, but this is an example of what would confront any government—national or local—that attempted to introduce a land value based tax today.

Henry George met with much opposition after his *Progress and Poverty* became more widely read, not only from the obvious landed interests, but also from no less an authority than the Pope.

During the 1886 election campaign for mayor of New York he enjoyed the encouragement of Father Edward McGlynn, a popular catholic priest, who supported George's ideas, despite them being contrary to Catholic doctrine. The Catholic view was in favour of the individual's right to private property and saw the land value tax as verging on socialism, which was anathema to the Catholic Church. McGlynn's persistent Georgist views led to his excommunication in 1887 (which was not revoked until 1892). A year earlier the Pope had issued an encyclical, Rerum Novarum, which dealt with economic issues and which supported private property in land; completely opposed to the Georgist land value tax. George subsequently wrote an open letter to the Pope in an appeal to modify his views, but without success.[15]

According to Prof Mason Gaffney, in a paper written in 2000, the 1891 Rerum Novarum 'remains basic to Catholic thought on economic justice today.'[16]

In Britain in the first decade of the 20th century similar struggles took place (see Chapter 4). Instead of the Pope, the opponents were the Lords Spiritual and Temporal, who also understood whence a large source of their income derived. At the turn of the 20th century the landowners were powerful, though few in number. But now their ranks have been swollen by the increased number of homeowners, who are also landowners on however modest a scale. Wightman notes, 'It is the UK's growing middle classes who are the new lairds.'[17] And so, they (we?) also have a vested interest in the collection of the economic rent through increased house prices, which may be realised at any point of sale, or borrowed against as collateral. Thus, the forces that would logically be ranged against LVT are now widespread and will need to be placated rather than confronted if LVT is to have any chance of general acceptance.

A contemporary example of landowners protecting their interests was demonstrated during the parliamentary enquiry into Land-Value Capture, which took place in 2018.[18] Evidence was collected from many interested parties, and one of the issues raised was in relation to Section 5 of the 1961 Land Compensation Act, mentioned earlier. Representatives of planning and environmental groups recommended that this section should be revoked, pointing out for example that the post-war new towns and garden cities were only made possible by local authorities being able to purchase land at or near existing use value.

Despite this argument, the representatives of developers and land agents protested that removal of this provision would be unfair to the landowners, describing such a proposal as 'iniquitous' and 'contrary to the British sense of fair play'. They even went so far as to suggest that to take such action would be contrary to the European Convention on Human Rights.[19] This is perhaps a good indication of the depth of belief in private property in land and the lengths to which landowners will go to preserve their interests.

General Resistance to Wealth Taxes

It may be of interest to moralists and the HMRC how wealth is acquired, but in general for the purposes of land value taxation it simply has to be there. There is general agreement that the wealthy should be taxed more highly than the less wealthy, so the wealthy spend no little effort in disguising their wealth or devising clever schemes to keep it from the hands of the tax collector. One of these ploys is to spread the idea that the taxation of wealth is in itself immoral, or at least unfair. They would argue that everyone has the right to keep the proceeds of their own hard work, skill and industry. For the state to demand even a part of this amounts to confiscation of private property, and it should find other means of raising revenue. The weakness of this argument is that others may equally apply their hard work, skill and industry to the best of their ability, but still end up with a great deal less wealth.

The resistance to wealth taxes is strong not just among the wealthy but also the less wealthy who hope one day that their fortunes will improve. As previously noted, the ability to pay objection is also invoked by the rich. In a paper on LVT in Vancouver, Christopher England noted, in regard to the issue of land forfeited due to LVT,

> Those unable to pay were not the poor, but rather extraordinarily wealthy individuals who had overextended themselves in urban real estate and were thus short on liquid assets.[20]

If the principle of imposing taxes in proportion to the level of wealth available is accepted, the problem remains: how to measure that wealth and therefore the ability to pay. Land values provide a means of making that measurement by distinguishing areas of relative prosperity on the basis of location. More prosperous areas are wealthier, therefore more able to bear a tax. Moreover, this prosperity is created by the hard work, skill and industry of the whole of society, and is not due solely to the efforts of any particular person or organisation on any particular site.

Despite the fairness implicit in this system, property taxes remain perhaps the most unpopular form of wealth tax. There is something sacrosanct about private property, whether land or buildings, that is jealously protected. Income tax, on the other hand, is about money, which is a substitute for wealth not yet realised and perhaps less subject to personal attachment. Also, it is easier for people to understand the built-in fairness of income tax: the more you earn, the more you pay and this seems to be more acceptable. Vickers makes the point that,

> Homeowners are a powerful lobby group and prefer to see their income and expenditure taxed than their wealth.[21]

The great weakness of income tax is that the more you *work* the more you pay, but this does not seem to register with most taxpayers as a disincentive. It would appear to be a question of education; a subject dealt with in the next section.

Historically, where direct taxes are concerned, income taxes became more popular with governments from the beginning of the 20th century and rapidly overtook the land value tax, which was struggling to become established at the same time.

Lack of Understanding of the Principles of LVT

All tax systems are supported to a greater or lesser degree by some theoretical justification in the attempt to make them acceptable to the taxpayer. It is generally more difficult to justify direct taxes such as income or property taxes as they are more readily personalised. Consequently, indirect taxes (VAT and travel taxes etc.,) are always more popular with politicians, for they can usually be disguised as higher prices, which apply generally and are not directed specifically at the individual. So, where direct taxes such as LVT are concerned it is important that the taxpayers are sufficiently persuaded before the tax is imposed.

All tax revenues, have to derive ultimately from existing wealth or the wealth-creation process. Taxing individuals or organisations that have little or no wealth is not only unjust but unproductive. It is commonly accepted that wealth is represented by the ownership of goods, property, or the means of production. The wealth-creation process is represented by work, manufacture and trade. In the process of (material) wealth creation, the following principal stages may be identified, in the sequence as they arise—in the diagrams of Chapter 2:

- Work on Land: This is the essential first step of any material production, with land being defined as any natural resource.
- Division of Labour (specialisation): This increases the effectiveness of any labour and the range and quality of produce.
- Education and Skill: This input increases the efficiency of specialisation.
- Investment (of capital): This enables greater enterprise towards more ambitious wealth creation, and naturally brings into play banking, saving and shareholding.

All of these contribute to wealth creation, and as noted in Chapter 1, where taxation is concerned, it is better to inhibit them as little as possible. This is why I emphasise taxing the end result—wealth—rather than the process. So, how can we justify taxing land, which is not in itself wealth?

We have to constantly remember that the proposition is not about imposing a tax on land but on land values, which are purely an indicator of the beneficial ownership of one of the essential elements of wealth creation. It is necessary to understand that land, like money, is not wealth, and that wealth may exist without money, but not without land.

Land therefore is more essential than money, but both can be readily exchanged for real wealth at any time that there is a demand. In the case of land, as with most other things, it is the demand that creates the value. As the demand increases the value increases, without any input of labour. For this reason, the ownership of land may be seen as an existing wealth asset.

Land values provide a clear gradation of measurement of the capacity for wealth creation by the tenant and therefore the degree to which wealth may be extracted by the landowner as land rent. LVT does not touch the tenant's wealth creation activity. What it does do is redirect the portion extracted as rent away from the landowner into the public purse.

Opponents of LVT would say this amounts to confiscation, but I hope I have explained above why it is not. Neither is LVT about eliminating private landownership or nationalising land; it is about nationalising the economic rent of land. The tax would be imposed in proportion to the surplus location values for each site—the values that register above the margin of production. Those occupying sites below the margin would not be taxed; whatever product they achieved they would keep.

With regard to income tax: however unpopular it may be, one of its strengths is that it is easily understood. Through the PAYE system it is largely paid in advance, automatically, so taxpayers do not have to go through the disagreeable business of finding the money later. This idea of payment at source was introduced in the UK in 1803 by the then prime minister Addington, and it has proved successful ever since as a way of avoiding disputes and objections. There is no reason why a similar system could not be applied to LVT where the site values are known in advance.

Perhaps even more unpopular are property taxes, such as the council tax, but the council tax is accepted because people understand the necessity to finance local services. They are willing to recognise that the level of payment is related to the capital value of their house, an implicit acknowledgement of the principle of ability to pay. What people appear to have difficulty understanding is that the value of their house is determined not only by its size and quality but also by where it is located. Separating the building value from the site value is crucial to any implementation of LVT. Collier sounds an optimistic note on LVT in saying,

> It is never too late to introduce such a tax. The electorate is far better educated than it was in Henry George's day, and so it should be easier to

build a political coalition that overcomes the resistance of vested interests.[22]

It is worth noting the current political interest in land value capture[23] and it is encouraging to see that people are readily able to understand that there should be a financial return to the public due to publicly funded infrastructure. But land value capture is confined only to these one-off events and is short-term. However, it is not a large step to understanding that land values are created not only by infrastructure projects but also other influences, and LVT takes account of all of these on a permanent basis.

Political Resistance

There has always been political resistance to land reform. Historically, in Britain, the politicians were very often the great landowners, who naturally did not want to jeopardise their primary source of wealth in any way. In the early years of our democracy, a qualification for being allowed to stand for parliament was the necessity to own property, which often meant property in land. In the early 20th century this allocation of power began to change with the extension of the franchise and the introduction of Liberal and then Labour-party reforms. But it was still not sufficient to get the land value tax proposals through parliament in 1909; the landowners' representation was still too powerful.

A good example of political collusion against land reform is given in Antonia Swinson's book, *Root of All Evil*, in which she refers to the so-called Second Domesday Book of 1873, which recorded the titles of ownership of all land in Britain and Ireland. It revealed that all of the land was owned by only 4.2% of the population, showing the landowners in a very bad light and consequently the report, 'was quietly buried from the view of academics and historians for over one hundred and thirty years.'[24] Not until 2001 was the existence of this document publicly admitted, and only due to the diligence of Kevin Cahill in researching for his book *Who Owns Britain*. According to Cahill, the Second Domesday Book was compiled within four years. In contrast, the modern Land Registry, which was started in 1925 with the introduction of the new Land Registration Act, is still only 85% complete—after 97 years. One may well ask, is there some lack of political will?

Another more recent example of a political cover-up is recorded by Chloe Timperley in her book *Generation Rent*. She refers to a report on taxation submitted to the government by Lord Stern who headed the Government Economic Service between 2003 and 2007. The report was 'buried in the chancellor's drawer' and 'never saw the light of day.'[25] In an article written for the *Financial Times* in 2014 Lord Stern revealed that, in the report, he had recommended the adoption of LVT. Timperley also records that Fred Harrison, a long-time LVT advocate, made a Freedom of Information request for publication, but was told that the government could 'neither confirm nor deny the report's existence'[26]

In 1931, the Labour government incorporated LVT in the Finance Act of that year, but the initiative was reversed by the succeeding Tory-majority coalition that represented landed interests. This pattern was repeated after the war, with the Labour government's attempts to capture 'betterment' value always being revoked by the succeeding Tory administration (see Chapter 4, *20th Century History*). For the best part of the 20th century, political resistance to land reform came from the political right, but with the increase of home ownership in recent decades vested interests in land ownership have become more widespread. At the beginning of the 20th century there were a small number of large landholders, now there are a large number of small landholders, the homeowners, of which, I hasten to add, I am one.

Figure 14 of Chapter 7 shows that homeownership reached a peak of 70% around 2000–2005. It has since declined but still represents a large number of voters with an interest in ever-rising house prices. Politicians are very aware of this interest group and are reluctant to alienate them by being seen to support a land value tax system that would threaten their increasing asset value. Although many progressive politicians are aware of the land value tax option for raising revenue, they are also very cautious about giving it their support for fear of a voter backlash. Those who know there is a problem are loath to be associated with anything bearing the dreaded word 'tax' in its title. For this reason, they tend towards the more anodyne 'land value capture' proposals, which have been tried in various forms for the last 70 years, but to little avail. For many politicians LVT is a tax that dare not speak its name.

Academic Resistance

Although Henry George was a journalist rather than an academic, his theories gave rise to a great deal of academic debate, for and against. Those against were generally of the neoclassical school, which held that land was just another form of capital. This notion was very much to the advantage of the large landowners, for it transformed the economic rent of land into no more than the legitimate interest on capital. The idea is of course antithetical to LVT, which is based on the original classical separation of land from labour and capital. In the book, *The Corruption of Economics,* Mason Gaffney reveals how neoclassical economics originated in the USA in the 1890s, specifically as a counter to the growing Georgist movement at that time.[27] The neoclassical view, however, prevailed in the academic world. Georgism was deliberately suppressed and several generations of economists have since been trained to treat LVT and Georgist ideas as no more than a historical curiosity (see Appendix 1).

The neoclassical view dominated later 20th-century economic policies and evolved, in the 1980s, into the neoliberal ideas that rely on the 'marketplace' to solve all economic problems. So there is considerable inertia in the academic world against anything that would question the neoclassical position. This view persists, despite the testimony of a number of eminent economists who have expressed their support for LVT over the years.[28] Nevertheless, since the financial crash of 2007–08, many cracks have begun to show in the current economic model, and a number of academics are looking again at the Henry George solution—an encouraging sign.

Politicians naturally turn to academics for guidance on economic matters, so the academics bear a heavy responsibility to get their theories right, as far as they are able. They have to be right for the whole of the populace, not just for those with vested interests. In his book, *Silent Theft*, David Bollier describes the situation in certain universities in the US engaged in research work, financed by private corporations, as distressing, and comments that,

> The marketisation of the academy is eroding its historic commitment to the public interest.[29]

Thankfully, the majority of academics are aware of the necessity to maintain their integrity, but there is always the temptation for this to be compromised when their institution is financed by wealthy donors with very different standards and different aims. As with politicians, private business interests are always eager to dignify their activities with academic support, but as Sayer notes,

> The powerful invoke economic theories only in so far as they suit them.[30]

CHAPTER 10

WHICH TAXES?

.

Where you find the laws most numerous, there you will find also the greatest injustice.

Arcesilaus (316–241 BC): Greek sceptic philosopher

10.1 The Single Tax Issue

Amongst economists who know about the land value tax, the term is often synonymous with *The Single Tax,* for that was seen as the main characteristic in the early days of its manifestation. In his book *Progress and Poverty*, Henry George proposed that the land value tax should be the only tax. This single tax idea has been identified with the LVT movement ever since, and is still insisted upon by the purists, but in recent years it has been questioned more and more. The purists are those who will not brook any modification of what they believe to be one of George's basic principles, as set out in *Progress and Poverty*, in which he explicitly proposes to 'abolish all taxation save that upon land values.'[1]

But Henry George was not the originator of the notion of the single tax: Over a hundred years earlier, the French Physiocrats propagated the idea which, in the mid-18th century, would have been based on an agrarian economy. Also, in 1775, Thomas Spence gave a lecture to the Newcastle Philosophical Society, in which he proposed that the land rent, paid to the parish, should be the only tax. In the introduction to his book, *The Pioneers of Land Reform*, written in 1920, the political historian Max Beer, makes the claim that, 'Spence must be regarded as the author of the Single Tax'.[2]

The idea arose again in America in the 1840s (when George was still a boy), with the advent of organised agrarian protests and the establishment of the National Reform Association, the members of which freely discussed the single-tax idea. In an interesting paper on the single tax written in 2007, Prof. Mark Lause suggests that George was strongly influenced in his early years in San Francisco by the members of the Reform movement. He comments, 'The idea of a single graduated tax on land emerged from reformers of that time and place.'[3] He notes also that, despite this, after the publication of *Progress and Poverty* in 1879, George continued 'to present himself as the originator of the Single Tax...'[4]

In an article published in *Land and Liberty* magazine, in the 2019 Summer issue, Edward Dodson notes that in the 1888 presidential election campaign, George gave his support to the Democratic candidate who, like George, was a free trader. For this reason, he was subsequently expelled from the United Labor Party. They accused him of 'abandoning the greater principle of the single tax for the lesser one of free trade.'[5]

This casts some doubt on the image of Henry George as the leading purveyor of the single tax—a role in which he is usually portrayed.

In any case we live in a very different world now to that of George's time. Purely in the world of transport, for example, we can travel around the globe in a matter of hours rather than months. Information is available to us almost instantaneously, rather than through the laborious Morse code—the medium for the telegraph system of the 1870s. We have instant access to the libraries of the world on our computers, and in the world of finance great fortunes can be made in microseconds, through electronic means, by clever operators who contribute nothing to the economies within which they operate. It is unlikely that George even had access to a telephone. The first telephone exchange was not established in San Francisco until 1878, by which time he had virtually completed his book *Progress and Poverty*.

In George's day taxes were few in number. The only significant taxes were federal excise duties and real-estate taxes, at the state level. The majority of present-day taxes did not arrive until the 20th century. So, the idea of a single tax was probably not such a drastic proposition then as it would be today. But apart from the great differences since George's time, my own opposition to the single tax is a matter of principle, which involves the issue of *site-dependence*.

In Chapter 1, in the section dealing with taxation according to means, I suggest the best forms of taxation are direct taxes, and those aimed at existing wealth. LVT satisfies both of these requirements, but as the name implies, it is limited in scope to the economic relationship that society has with land, especially urban land. I hope it is made clear in the explanations of Chapter 2 that the bulk of any revenue derived from LVT would be from higher value urban sites. In large part the enterprises that occupy these sites are there through necessity; dictated by the need to be close to the centre of economic activity. They are essentially 'site-dependent': the high street shop, the department store, the central office, the bank. All need a central site in order to operate effectively. There are, however, other enterprises and individuals who are less site-dependent, who are nevertheless able to generate high earnings through activities that have no need to be permanently located on high-value sites.

In his book *Daylight Robbery* Dominic Frisby describes the phenomenon of the 'digital nomad', who may prosper without any need of a permanent base: 'You can work in the digital economy from anywhere.'[6] A skilled operator can work effectively at home, or trading from a laptop in a hotel room, purely as an agent, without any need for an office, display space or close proximity to any centre of population. One thinks also of high-earning individuals in the areas of sport and entertainment, who are able to amass considerable fortunes but who are highly mobile. They take their skills with them. They do not need a fixed site. Under a single-tax system, those who are not site-dependent, though they may have amassed considerable wealth, would be virtually free of tax. How then, in satisfaction of the first principle cited in Chapter 1 would they make their contribution to the society from which they benefit? To say that they would pay tax through the site value of where they live is not sufficient; that applies to everyone. No doubt they all do useful work, but why should the burden of tax fall only on those who are site-dependent?

The most site-dependent of all economic activities is that of farming, and yet, as we have seen, the agricultural sector is always at the margin in the hierarchy of land values and would not account for any great amount of revenue in any system of LVT. At the present time some of the most lucrative economic activities have very little need of any high-value central site from which to operate successfully. The advent of the internet has enabled the creation of new enterprises such as Amazon, Google and Facebook, which have proved to be highly successful and very lucrative sources of wealth generation. For them, the use of the ether is probably more important than the use of the land. Frisby notes that 'Amazon became the West's biggest retailer without owning a single shop.'[7] The CEOs of these businesses are now amongst the top ten richest individuals on the planet.[8] Certainly, all these individuals ought to be well rewarded for their enterprise and initiative, but if one accepts the principle of 'ability to pay', it is difficult to see how a land value tax would measure their ability to make the appropriate contribution towards the society from which their great wealth has been created. One must respect their generosity through philanthropic giving, but society should not have to be dependent on private philanthropy for its proper functioning.

In another aspect of new technology, Frisby offers an interesting explanation of the crypto-currencies, originally designed as a libertarian device to preserve the privacy of transactions and to avoid government control over taxation and regulation.[9] None of the crypto-currency activities are site-dependent, but they are nevertheless capable of generating great fortunes, which would be beyond the reach of LVT. These are questions that cannot be avoided, and my own view is that there has to be some other form of tax that would address these anomalies.

The ideal would be a straightforward wealth tax that would tax the final accumulations of wealth rather than the means of achieving them. But the difficulty with this is the age-old problem of identification and measurement: there are many clever ways that accumulations of wealth may be hidden through trusts, secret bank accounts and offshore havens. Such a wealth tax could replace income tax, capital gains tax and inheritance tax, and it could be applied separately to individuals or companies. But all of this is a complex area, which would require much careful planning and would no doubt merit a separate book.

On this particular issue, the government established a Wealth Tax Commission in 2020 to examine the feasibility of introducing a wealth tax for the UK.[10] In its report, in December 2020, it suggested that a one-off wealth tax was feasible but not a permanent annual wealth tax, the apparent reason being a matter of implementation. The one-off method would be easier to value and measure and would not provide the opportunity to prepare avoidance schemes. The report was about practicality; the issue of justice was barely mentioned. This amounts to the rather depressing admission that the government can always be outwitted by those having great wealth to preserve; they will always have the means to escape being proportionally taxed. It is much more pragmatic to tax those with modest wealth, even the poor. They are the easy unmoving targets.

More recently, and on a more optimistic note, the University of Greenwich has published a paper, 'The case for a progressive annual wealth tax in the UK'.[11] In the conclusion the paper states: 'The case for progressive wealth taxes is built on the need to tackle and reduce wealth inequality' and also 'that a progressive wealth tax… has the potential to raise huge revenues.'

However, I still believe it is a matter of political will; the government could adapt some scheme to tax the very wealthy if it really wanted to.

In the meantime, we have to work with what we've got, and the next best thing for dealing with these accumulations, I suggest, would be some modified form of income tax. All taxes are unpopular, but income tax is generally accepted as fair, in that it is at least progressive. Perhaps one could retain the income tax with an entry threshold of say £50,000. That would exempt the majority of earners, whilst dealing with the rest progressively, at the same time recognising that most private wealth accumulations arise from those on higher incomes, or are the result of unearned interest from surplus wealth.

There are other taxes that might also be retained; the so-called social taxes, which are designed as much to influence behaviour as to gain a source of revenue.

The 'sin taxes' on alcohol, smoking and gambling, and the 'eco-taxes' on fuel and carbon emissions are amongst these, which even the LVT purists might consider keeping. So perhaps the idea of a single tax is already an anachronism.

The opponents of LVT would, I believe, jump on the term 'single tax' with glee. Perhaps a better title would be 'essential tax' or 'first tax', but to insist on it being the only tax would not help in getting the idea of LVT accepted by the ordinary voter; the immediate challenge for the LVT movement is in getting LVT understood, accepted and implemented.

Many contemporary academics, politicians and influential journalists, who are otherwise supporters of the idea of LVT, baulk at the idea of the single tax, and I believe they are correct in their caution. The single-tax issue may yet be the greatest obstacle to overcome for LVT advocates, who clearly need to face up to this problem within their own ranks. The single tax may have been feasible in George's time when economic structures were much simpler, but in the complex contemporary world 140 years later, it is in my view more realistic to accept the need for other taxes, or other means for capturing an appropriate contribution towards society from those who may create great wealth from situations that are not necessarily land related. My own feeling is that if Henry George were with us today and able to observe the complexity and sophistication of contemporary society, he would be more than willing to modify the single-tax constraint.

Box 2. On Libertarian Support for LVT

It is perhaps surprising to many liberals, and those on the centre left of politics, to find that many libertarians also support the idea of a land value tax. A possible explanation for this, I suggest, lies with the early Georgist proposal for the single tax, where all other taxes are eliminated. The most basic characteristic of libertarianism is the idea of 'minimum government', which generally translates as minimum taxes. When taken to its extreme expression it becomes anarchism—ideally no taxes at all. In the US, libertarians who support this version of LVT describe themselves as geo-libertarians. One of the fiercest opponents of LVT was Murray Rothbard (1926–95), a former libertarian leader and member of the Austrian school of economics. He later went on to be a founder of the movement known as anarcho-capitalism. Todd Altman, a leading geo-libertarian in the US has written an interesting explanation of the geo-libertarian position, which also includes a refutation of Rothbard's view of LVT.[12]

10.2 Taxes to Eliminate, Reduce or Keep

In Chapter 1, on basic principles, I suggest that it is better to impose taxes on existing wealth rather than the wealth-creation process, and also that, in general, direct taxes are more honest than indirect taxes (often described as stealth taxes). This sub-section brings these strands together under the question of which taxes might be eliminated, reduced or maintained within a system where LVT plays a significant part.

Prior to the 20th century, taxes in Britain were few in number. In the 1870s customs and excise duties still accounted for 60% of government revenue, income tax about 8%. Historically, governments had always raised money through borrowing from private individuals or banks in order to fund wars (so establishing the national debt).

The introduction of the income tax in 1799 was intended as a temporary measure to fund the Napoleonic wars. Everyone was against it, and for the best part of the 19th century politicians on both sides made many promises to abolish it. But the income tax was difficult to shake off, as we all know. There was, of course, no welfare state as we know it today. Poor relief was obtained through the old poor-law acts of 1601, which were financed through local taxes at parish level—the 'rates.' The proliferation of the many different forms of taxation we know today occurred mainly in the 20th century due to the advent of the welfare state, and the need to finance the growing demand for social services. These taxes are now both numerous and complex and the contemporary tax regime does not seem to readily conform with any of Adam Smith's four maxims, let alone that of certainty. It is difficult now for most ordinary taxpayers to grasp the convoluted workings of the income-tax system without resort to expert advice or guesswork. There is undoubtedly a need for simplification, if only to provide people with a clear understanding of what taxes they are expected to pay.

In 2008 the Office for Budget Responsibility (OBR) published its 'Sources of Government Revenue' forecast for 2008–09, which showed up to 20 different sources. In July 2010 HM Treasury established ~~The~~ Office of Tax Simplification (OTS) for the purpose of reducing the complexities of the tax system for both business and individuals. In 2019 OBR published its forecast for 2019–20 which showed an increase to 24 sources (see Table 4). So it isn't clear to me what the OTS had achieved in that 11-year period.

So what should be done?

I believe that the introduction of LVT would provide a clear and unambiguous source of revenue that could be used to enable the reduction or elimination of other existing taxes—but which taxes?

Table 4, taken from the Office for Budget Responsibility data, shows the forecast for 2019–20 for government tax receipts from all sources. There are a total of 24, which are listed in descending order of the percentage of revenue raised.

Income tax tops the list followed by national insurance and VAT. These three account for 64% of all revenue, far more than the other 21 sources combined. So clearly, they are very significant.

	Source & Type	%	Suggested Action
1.	Income tax (D)	27.3	Keep but reduce and combine with NIC
2.	NIC (D & I)*	19.0	Keep but reduce and combine with income tax
3.	VAT (I)	17.8	Abolish or reduce

	Source & Type	%	Suggested Action
4.	Corporation tax (I)	6.9	Replace with 'Full Inclusion Tax' and reduce
5.	Council tax (D)	4.5	Replace with LVT
6.	Business rates (I)	3.9	Replace with LVT
7.	Fuel duties (I)	3.8	Abolish or Reduce
8.	Other taxes and royalties	3.3	? (see comment below)
9.	Stamp duty (D)	2.1	Abolish
10.	VAT refunds	2.0	Related to VAT collection efficiency
11.	Alcohol duties (I)	1.6	Keep (a social tax)
12.	Tobacco duties (I)	1.2	Keep (a social tax)
13.	Capital gains tax (D)	1.2	Abolish
14.	Other HMRC Taxes**	1.0	Keep social or eco-taxes; see also comment below
15.	Vehicle excise duties (I)	0.8	Replace with road pricing
16.	Inheritance tax (D)	0.7	Keep, with increased threshold
17.	Insurance-premium tax (I)	0.6	Abolish or reduce in line with VAT
18.	Air-passenger duties (I)	0.5	Keep (an eco-tax)
19.	Stamp duty on shares (D)	0.4	See comment below
20.	Apprenticeship levy(I)	0.4	Keep for as long as required
21.	Bank levy (I)	0.3	See comment below

Source & Type		%	Suggested Action
22.	Climate-change levy (I)	0.3	Keep (an eco-tax)
23..	Bank surcharge (I)	0.2	See comment below
24.	Soft drinks levy (I)	0.1	Keep (a social tax)
Key: (D) Direct Tax (I) Indirect Tax			

* The employee's share of NIC contributions are direct, the employer's share indirect.
** Includes customs duties, betting and gaming duties, landfill tax and aggregates levy

Table 4. UK Government Tax Receipts for 2019–20

(Source: Office for Budget Responsibility, Economic and Fiscal outlook for 2019–20)

In the table, the column headed 'suggested action' represents my suggestions as to which taxes might be abolished, replaced or kept. This I found surprisingly difficult to decide. Although I tried to be objective, I daresay my own view is no better or worse than anyone else's. Perhaps you might like to compile your own list of preferences? In addition to the suggestions I have made, here are some further comments about some of the taxes:

Income Tax and NIC

If only to simplify administration, there is a good argument for combining income tax and NIC into one tax, which could be much reduced, and with a higher entry threshold.

VAT

VAT is a Europe-wide tax. Now that Britain has left the European Union it could be reduced or abolished altogether. Britain adopted VAT on joining the EU; it replaced the old purchase tax. In Australia VAT is known as GST, a goods and services tax, applied at a rate of 10%, considerably less than the rate of VAT in Europe. There is no VAT in the USA, but a sales tax on goods and services (the inverse of a purchase tax), applied at state and, often, local levels.

Corporation Tax

Corporation tax is very vulnerable to avoidance and is a problem in all countries. It is a tax on manufacturers and trade and ideally should be abolished or reduced, but it needs to be agreed internationally to avoid retaliation from other countries competing for business investment. An interesting article on the Schumpeter blog of the *Economist,* dated 15 March 2013, describes two possible alternatives to the Corporation Tax: the 'Unitary Tax' and the 'Full Inclusion Tax'. The latter would appear to have several advantages and should be seriously considered as a replacement.[13]

Council Tax and Business Rates

Council tax and business rates are property taxes and ideal candidates for replacement by a local site value tax (see Chapter 3, Application of LVT).

Fuel Duties

Fuel duties should be abolished or reduced, as they are a tax on transport that affects everyone adversely. But they are also seen as a deterrent to carbon emissions – so a balance has to be found. Perhaps they could be absorbed into a system of road pricing.

Other Taxes and Royalties

In the OBR data these are noted as: licence fee receipts, environmental levies, EU/ETS auction receipts, Scottish taxes, diverted profits tax and other taxes. Under suggested action I have unsurprisingly left a question mark. They are not necessarily all taxes, but other sources of revenue, but they account for a substantial 3.3% of all receipts.

Stamp Duty

Stamp duty (officially, but rather misleadingly known as Stamp Duty Land Tax for historic reasons) is a tax on trade and increases the cost of housing. It should be abolished.

Capital gains Tax

Capital Gains Tax should be abolished. One of the main purposes of this tax is to recoup the (unearned) increase in value of properties on resale, but this could be done more effectively through a land value tax.

Other HMRC Taxes

The social and eco-taxes could be kept. Customs duties are subject to international negotiation; they are a free/fair trade issue.

Stamp Duty on Shares

Stamp duty on shares could be included in a general reform of financial transactions to combat unproductive speculation in currencies and shares, short selling and other predatory practices. It is a complex area, which would require international co-operation and is beyond the scope of this book, but it exercises an increasing number of reformist organisations, which seek to bring under control the 'wild-west' world of finance, in which taxes play a large part.

Bank Levy and Bank Surcharge

The Bank levy was imposed after the economic collapse of 2007–08, as a sort of repayment for the bank bailouts (a punishment tax?). For that reason, most people would think it justifiable. The Bank Surcharge was introduced in 2016 as an extra tax on bank profits, but only brings in 0.1% of total revenue. There seems to be a clear need for rationalisation of corporation tax, bank levy and bank surcharge in the question of how to tax banking activity.

Inheritance tax

Finally, I would single out inheritance tax as a rather special case. It is true that it does not rank highly on the list of revenue earners, but it raises strong feelings for and against. Those who are opposed say it should be abolished altogether; why after all should those who have worked hard all their lives not be allowed to leave what wealth they have to their children without being penalised by a tax?—A good point with which I have much sympathy. However, there has always been a strong counter argument, where large amounts of wealth are inherited: Why should some be allowed to inherit a fortune, which could enable them to live well the rest of their lives without ever having to do a stroke of work? The current system, with a threshold of £325,000 is a compromise, but is probably insufficiently generous. This threshold could be raised to £500,000 or even £1million, which would seem a decent amount for anyone to inherit. These figures are always a matter of debate, and in any case should always be subject to revision, due to inflation.

I suggest that whatever loss of revenue may be incurred from eliminating or reducing any of the above taxes could be made good from a new land value tax. In all cases, gains and losses have to be graduated over a transition period, and the principle of tax neutrality respected.

Those hard-line Georgists who still insist on the single tax would presumably eliminate all 24—a difficult proposition to imagine. One suspects they might be willing to compromise on some of them.

CHAPTER 11

WELFARE

Amid the greatest accumulations of wealth, men die of starvation, and puny infants suckle dry breasts.

Henry George (1839–1897):
American political economist

Apart from the funding of public services, a great deal of taxation is related to the funding of benefits that come under the heading of welfare, designed basically to help those on low incomes, or in economic distress for whatever reason.

Table 5 below shows 14 different forms of current benefits (including the state pension). Some of these are aimed at the actual alleviation of poverty. Others are allowances available to all income groups. It is quite difficult to know where poor relief ends and welfare begins, or indeed, how to define welfare. We tend not to see education or health care as part of a welfare system but more as social services, akin to a police force or a sanitation system. Perhaps pensions should be seen in the same way. Furthermore, state pensions are not free.

As with national health they are largely funded by the NIC contributions through the working life of the pensioner, so it is curious to see them included as welfare.

Benefit	£ bn.	%
State pension	96.7	43.36
Tax credits	22.8	10.22
Housing benefits	20.2	9.06
Disability living allowance	18.8	8.43
Incapacity benefits	15.0	6.72
Child benefit	11.6	5.20
Other allowances*	8.5	3.81
Universal credit	8.0	3.81
Attendance allowance	5.7	2.56
Carer's allowance	2.9	1.30
Maternity/Paternity payments	2.7	1.21
Winter fuel payments	2.0	0.89
Income support	1.9	0.85
Jobseeker's allowance	1.3	0.58

* Includes other NI social security, tax-free childcare and other DWP payments.

Table 5. UK Government Welfare Spending, 2018–19

(Source: OBR, Economic and Fiscal Outlook, March 2019, CPSO p. 100.)

Before discussing the issue of welfare, it is worth noting how it arose historically out of the old poor laws that, in England, began in the 14th century. Prior to that, poor relief was only available through the auspices of the church, which was required (by the Rule of St. Benedict) to provide hospitals for the sick and elderly and hospitality for travellers. In addition, wealthy benefactors provided almshouses for the relief of the poor, which in the early years were supervised by the church. The government (the king) was not directly involved. It was a feudal system, where the peasants had no rights—certainly not the right to be prosperous. The initial involvement of the government was designed more to constrain or punish the poor than to help them. The following account summarises the main events in chronological order:

Evolution of Poor Relief to Welfare in England:

1349. The Ordinance of Labourers, under Edward III, designed to cap wages and food prices due to a labour shortage after the Black Death.

1351. The Statute of Labourers placed restrictions on the movement of labourers.

1495. The Vagabonds and Beggars Act, under Henry VIII, punished vagrants with the stocks. Sturdy beggars were punished and moved on.

1531. The Vagabonds Act replaced the stocks with whipping for the able bodied. The 'impotent poor' (the disabled, sick or elderly) were allocated an official area in which to beg.

1536. The dissolution of the monasteries removed many hospitals and almshouses, the primary sources of poor relief, and caused greater hardship.

1547. The Vagabond Act introduced under Edward VI, in which vagrants were punished by two years servitude and branded with a 'V' for the first offence, executed for the second.

1555. To deal with unemployment, Houses of Correction (an early form of workhouse), were introduced in London.

1563. The Act for the Relief of the Poor, under Elizabeth I, required all parish residents 'with the ability to pay' to contribute to poor-relief collections. This act recognised that the poor needed help rather than punishment.

1601. The Elizabethan Poor Law recognised for the first time the 'deserving poor', perhaps the first move away from seeing poverty as a crime. It established the funding at local level through the Rates—each parish was considered to be responsible for its own poor.

1662. The Poor Relief Act (the Settlement Act), allowed relief only to established parishioners—further reducing labour mobility.

1696. The first workhouse was established in Bristol, combining a house of correction with housing, work and care for the deserving poor.

1780. The Sunday School movement, first established in Gloucester, was a major advance in helping the poor. Financed privately and also by the church, it formed the basis for later universal education. The provision of education was seen as the best way to help the poor.

1782. The Thomas Gilbert Act established poor houses for the aged and infirm and 'outdoor relief' for the able bodied, presaging the 1796 Speenhamland system.[1] The Speenhamland system was an early form of Universal Basic Income, but was not universally adopted. A criticism was that it simply enabled the employers to pay lower wages.

1834. The Poor Law Amendment Act was not designed to help the poor but to ease the burden on ratepayers. It superseded the outdoor relief and Speenhamland systems and introduced workhouses, which were deliberately designed to provide worse conditions than those of the lowest paid labour. They were designed to be punitive—a retrogressive step.

1880. The Elementary Education Act made free school attendance for 5–10-year-olds compulsory, thereby involving the government in funding for education.

The new Liberal government of 1906 initiated the modern welfare state in Britain with a swathe of welfare measures prior to World War One: *

1906. Free school meals.

1908. Pensions for the over-70s.

1909. Labour exchanges for the unemployed and a minimum wage in certain industries.

1911. National Insurance for limited free medical treatment and sick pay.

1912. Shop-workers' half-day compensation scheme.

The post-war Conservative and Labour governments continued with reforms, but at a slower pace:

1925. Pension-entitlement ages reduced to 65 for men, 60 for women.

---

* The first modern welfare measures were introduced in Germany, ironically, by the anti-socialist Bismarck: Health insurance in 1883, accident insurance, in 1884, old-age and disability insurance in 1889.

1944. The Education Act introduced free secondary education to age 15 and facilitated access to higher education.

1948. The National Health Service, introduced by the Labour government, confirmed and consolidated the modern welfare state in Britain.

In England, perhaps the beginnings of the welfare system could be said to have started with the Poor-Law Acts of 1601. But these were funded from local rates rather than at the national level. For a long period, relief of the poor, other than through these poor-law arrangements, came from the church, charitable giving or individual benefactors. In the 19th century mutual and friendly societies were established to help people with housing, and the new trade unions assisted workers in times of hardship, but these movements were self-funded and independent—the government did not see itself as responsible for direct financial help for the poor.

The Poor Law Amendment Act of 1834, which introduced workhouses, still saw poverty more as a crime than a misfortune. But this attitude began to change in the second half of the 19th century, with an increasing awareness of the terrible conditions of the poor in a rapidly industrialising society. In 1880 the Elementary Education Act introduced the necessity for regular state funding, so the state inevitably became involved.

It is astonishing that even in the late 19th century many in the government that made the laws of the land, still believed that the existence of poverty was not their responsibility. The ensuing years witnessed a complete change of attitude. However, it was not until the 20th century that the modern welfare state really began to emerge with the reforming Liberal government of 1906.

All these measures of course, had to be funded, and in addition to the costs of rearmament for the forthcoming war, it put great pressure on the government to find new ways of raising revenue. The income tax played an ever-increasing role in this process. During the course of the 20th century, poor relief, as such, became absorbed into the new welfare system to the extent that, at the present time, certain benefits are no longer seen as necessary measures to assist the poor but as normal social rights. This has led to what is often described as the 'dependency culture'. Prior to the 20th century, most of these benefits, including pensions, did not exist. Were they to disappear, the majority of us would be plunged into great difficulty. So, if one also took into account free education and a national health service, only the very rich, even now, could be truly independent.

This issue of dependency resurrects the older discussions about liberty and freedom, which have been ongoing at least since the days of the Enlightenment. What role, if any, has the State to play in any of this?

This argument has to a large extent given rise to the so-called left and right of politics. Those on the left put their faith in centralised state control for the dispensation of justice and believe that freedom can only be gained through collective cooperation. Those on the right believe the opposite: that the state should only be involved with basic requirements, such as national defence and essential infrastructure; all other economic matters should be left to the free market and individual enterprise.

Between these two extremes are probably the majority of citizens who may not be persuaded either way. But despite the general increase in the standard of living since the dark days of the 19th century, they are still aware of widespread discontent, and the increasing maldistribution of wealth. Even in Britain, one of the wealthiest countries in the world, evidence of real poverty is returning, with the proliferation of food banks, in-work poverty, homelessness and the growing demands on welfare provision. It is generally agreed that these demands may be reduced simply by making people better off as individuals, and this is attempted through raising tax thresholds and imposing minimum wage levels. But these are only remedial measures, which do not deal with the basic causes of deprivation.

Henry George had a somewhat sceptical view of welfare, or 'charity' as it was better known in his time:

Charity cannot right a wrong; only justice can do that. Charity is false, futile and poisonous when offered as a substitute for justice.[2]

Although the modern welfare system has become necessary, not merely to alleviate poverty, but also to provide what are now seen as normal social services, there is an insight in George's view. The receipt of welfare can be demeaning, especially where means testing is concerned. It may even lead to downright cruelty: One of the conditions for terminally ill people applying for support under the new universal credit system is to 'prove that they are dying.'[3]

One of the main causes of deprivation amongst low-income groups is the cost of housing, hence the need for housing benefits or (proposed) new rent controls. A land value tax would have the effect of lowering house prices and consequently rents. This would be a much better way of helping low earners than housing benefit, which in any case goes straight into the pocket of the landlord without directly helping the tenant. Admittedly this would be a slow process, but far more effective in the long run.

Through the gradual transfer of wealth, an LVT would put money into the pockets of ordinary taxpayers and help them with many issues other than housing. But in the meantime, we have to have the welfare and benefits system, which would gradually become less necessary as the advantages of LVT began to take effect. It could be argued that pensions, free education, national-health provision and unemployment allowance are not welfare, but necessary services that could reasonably be expected in any advanced, progressive society.

CHAPTER 12

SUMMARY

> The law in its majestic equality forbids the rich as well as the poor to sleep under bridges, to beg in the streets and to steal bread.
>
> **Anatole France** (1884–1924): French poet and novelist

This chapter is simply a summary of the main points that have arisen in the book, which I list as follows:

1. First Principles
Applying to All Taxes

- Every able-bodied, able-minded adult who benefits from belonging to a society should make a contribution towards its upkeep.
- Such contribution should be in accordance with the ability to pay.

Applying to LVT

- LVT should be the tax of first resort.

- LVT must be a replacement tax and not an additional tax.
- Other necessary taxes may be kept, albeit reduced where possible.

2. Education

Acceptance of LVT will depend on public understanding of:

- Community-created value.
- Land values as an indication of collective prosperity, varying and measured (in the urban context) by location.
- All property values are composed of two parts, the value of the building and the value of the site.
- LVT is not about nationalisation of land, but nationalisation of the economic rent of land.
- There is a big difference between rural and urban land values; by far the greater proportion of revenue would be obtained from the urban situation.

3. Implementation

- To avoid disruption, LVT must be introduced gradually (over a period of at least 10 years).
- Before the introduction of LVT, a comprehensive revaluation—separating site from building values—would need to be carried out and thereafter regularly maintained.
- If applied at local level, LVT could readily replace the Council Tax and Business Rates.

- The change to LVT would create 'winners and losers', which is inevitable in correcting a long-standing injustice.

4. Effects of LVT

- LVT would help to resolve the housing crisis by restraining house prices.
- LVT would bring to an end land banking and speculation.
- If introduced nationally LVT would shift the burden of taxation off poorer areas onto wealthier areas, thereby resulting in a general transfer of wealth throughout the country.
- LVT would be impossible to avoid and therefore increase the efficiency of collection.

5. Land Ownership

- The legitimacy of land ownership is challenged in this book. However, as Henry George pointed out, it may continue provided the economic rent is surrendered to the public.

CHAPTER 13

DEFINITIONS

> The least-bad tax is the property tax on
> the unimproved value of land, the Henry
> George argument of many, many years ago.
>
> **Milton Friedman** (1912–2006),
> American Nobel economics laureate

The main purpose of this book has been to communicate
the ideas of LVT to those with no special knowledge
of economics, and therefore I have used terms and
meanings as they are generally understood in common
usage. However, there are, in certain cases, definitions
used by economists that have specific meanings and
need to be explained.

Wealth

As commonly understood, material wealth is considered
to be represented by the possession of goods, money,
land or natural resources. But this view is misleading.
Goods are certainly wealth, but money, land and natural
resources are not (see below).

Material wealth is only produced through a combination of labour applied to land (all natural resources). Land is only one of the elements of wealth production, not wealth itself. Natural resources remain only potential wealth until labour is applied.

Knowledge is also a form of wealth, which may be exchanged for money or goods. It is knowledge that provides the basis for the service industries.

It is necessary to appreciate these distinctions for a proper understanding of the principles behind the land value tax.

Money

Money is a deferred claim on wealth; it is not in itself wealth. It is a representation of wealth, the value of which depends entirely on the trust of society that it will be honoured as a medium of exchange. It also has value as a means of wealth storage. It may be exchanged for tangible wealth or for a service, at which point the deferment is passed on to the seller.

It is generally considered better if money has no intrinsic value. A problem in the past with gold and silver coins was that they were often clipped, and the clippings melted down to make duplicates.

Apart from notes and coins it does not need to exist physically. Notes and coins have largely been replaced by the electronic credit system, which is generally considered more convenient and efficient. Exchanges of money may take place by the alteration of figures on the account sheets of the parties concerned, or by electronic transfers, the accounts being stored in a computer memory. In every case it depends on the existence of trust.

Land

As generally understood, land is taken to be simply the dry surface of the earth on which we live and work. But for economists the definition extends to all natural resources: oil and minerals below ground, natural forests, fish in the sea, even the radio spectrum—in other words all the gifts of nature that are not man-made.

In Chapter 5, Resource Rents, I necessarily make this distinction. But for the purposes of land value taxation, in the urban context, the 'land' in question is not something tangible, but rather an abstraction: a two-dimensional area on the surface of the earth for the exclusive use of which any owner or occupier is liable to a charge.

Property/Real Estate

In the UK the word *property* is generally understood to refer to a building and the site upon which it stands, considered as one combined item. This is how it is used generally throughout this book, unless indicated otherwise. In the US the same combination is known as real estate.

Of course, where land value taxation is concerned the two elements have to be viewed separately, so one might speak of property in the land only or the building only, but this should be made clear if such is the case.

The word *property* is also used to describe any tangible object that a person or organisation may own. It is also employed in the intangible world of ideas, patents, copyright, trademarks etc., usually described as 'intellectual property'. This area is complex and problematic and best left for a separate discussion.

Earnings

Earnings are the direct reward for work done. Earnings may take the form of money, produce, manufactured items, modified natural resources, or any other form of wealth that may be exchanged for money. Where a return arises from a situation where no work is done (as with interest on savings), the return is considered to be 'unearned'.

Wages

Wages are that share of earnings paid to an employee by an employer, usually in the form of money, but they may also be in produce.

Capital

The word *capital* may be used in two different ways by economists and non-economists alike.

It is commonly employed to describe the total asset value of a person or a company; their total wealth is their capital. Where a property is concerned, the selling price is its capital value, determined at the point of exchange. The annual rental value 'capitalised' is a guide to its selling price.

The other definition of capital, more commonly used by economists, is 'that part of wealth used to create more wealth'. This second definition is somewhat more complicated.*

The workman's tools are his capital, the farmer's seeds are capital. Any tool or machine—even a whole factory—may be capital. However, it is more often represented by money, which is lent at interest to an entrepreneur to purchase the means to produce more wealth. This is the basis of the 'capitalist' system, in which the lenders are banks or investors looking for a return on their money.

Another form of capital is intellectual capital (or skill). A teacher's knowledge is his or her capital. It is another form of 'tool', which expedites the process of wealth creation and may be exchanged for a payment, as with any other form of labour.

Economic Rent

The most commonly understood meaning of 'rent' is the payment made to a landlord for a house or flat, or to a company for a hire-car or other equipment. This is known as 'contract rent', where an agreement is signed by both parties.

---

* The financial website Investopedia describes several types of investment capital: debt capital, equity capital, working capital and trading capital: refer to, https://www.investopedia.com/terms/c/capital.asp

The payment of a rent is for the use of something owned by another. This ownership may be extended to intangible things such as patents or monopolies, the owner of which can exact a payment for access by others. Economists may refer to 'monopoly rents', 'scarcity rents' or 'information rents', all of which allude to the ownership of some asset or advantage which may be exploited to gain an income—some form of economic rent.[1]

However, the term *economic rent* is generally understood to relate primarily to land, and it is only this form that I concentrate on in this book. As mentioned in Chapter 1, this economic rent (or the Law of Rent) was first described in Ricardo's book *On the Principles of Political Economy and Taxation*, in which he stated that the rent of land is 'that compensation which is paid to the owner of land for the use of its original and indestructible powers'.[2] He also noted 'rent is always the difference between the produce obtained by the employment of two equal quantities of capital and labour'.[3] Ricardo also identified the margin of land value, below which no rent could be exacted. His theory has been summarised thus:

> The rent of land is determined by the excess of its product over that which the same application can secure from the least productive land in use.[4]

In other words, for the same input of labour, sites of equal size will provide different levels of product because of some relative advantage (which in the agrarian situation is fertility or some other natural advantage).

It has to be remembered that Ricardo's theories were devised at a time when economic ideas were still based largely on an agrarian economy. But the Ricardian 'differential rent' may still be applied to the urban situation, where land values differ, according to their location.

Rentier

A rentier is a person who derives a rental income from an economic situation towards which he has made no contribution. A rental payment can be justified through the simple fact of ownership. Traditionally the word 'rentier' was applied to the absentee landowner and is of French origin.

APPENDIX 1

NEOCLASSICAL ECONOMICS

Perhaps the most effective continuous force ranged against LVT throughout the world has always been the neoclassical school of economic thought.

Neoclassical economics arose in the US in the late 19th century, almost concurrently with the rise of Georgism but represented a very different ideology where the status of land was concerned. Georgism continued the classical economic view that there were three basic elements leading to wealth creation which were separate and distinct: land, labour and capital. Henry George made these distinctions very clear and pointed out that the return to land was rent, the return to labour was wages and the return to capital was interest.[1]

The neoclassical view was that land was merely another form of capital and therefore only the two elements, labour and capital were significant. This view was advantageous for landowners and large industrialists who were able to claim their rightful return on capital—which now included land.

The political philosophy of Henry George was seen by the rich and powerful as a direct threat to their power base. In his book *The Corruption of Economics,* co-authored with Fred Harrison, Mason Gaffney comments,

> Henry George and his reform proposals were a clear and present political danger and challenge to the landed and intellectual establishments of the world. Few people realise to what degree the founders of neoclassical economics changed the discipline for the express purpose of deflecting George and frustrating future students seeking to follow his arguments.[2]

This opposition to George was seriously organised in the US. In an article on the Wealth and Want website, William Batt gives an account of the influence of the railroad and land 'barons' who, through their financial sponsorship of the major universities, were able to determine important placements of academic positions favourable to neoclassical economics.[3]

The early reformist movement in the US, in which Georgism played a leading part, became forgotten in the tumultuous events of the first half of the 20th century; two world wars and a major economic depression.

During this time the neoclassical school prevailed and came to dominate economic thought throughout the world. The neoclassical movement was centred in the US at the university of Chicago, which became known as The Chicago School. One of its leading exponents was the economist Milton Friedman, quoted in the epigram for Chapter 13 as a supporter of the idea of LVT. How does one explain this seeming paradox?

Having watched the video of the lecture in which he makes his statement of support[4], my only explanation is that Friedman was praising LVT because it is efficient and difficult to avoid—a view that most economists hold. However, in another interview[5] he advocates the use of digital currencies because they would make it more difficult for the government to collect taxes generally, a seemingly libertarian view that appears to contradict his earlier position. For me this remains a mystery.

The neoclassical school later evolved into neoliberalism, that puts its faith in free markets, deregulation and privatisation and which still holds sway today. But in recent years there have been signs that the neoclassical/neoliberal orthodoxy is being questioned as inequalities become more acute and the current system is seen to be working only for an ever-smaller elite.

The practice of LVT in various forms is still alive in the world, especially in Pennsylvania in the US, and there is evidence of a revival of interest amongst economists, journalists and academics worldwide.[6] At the political level, recent evidence of this revival comes from Germany where, in November 2020, the state of Baden-Württemberg elected to introduce a land value tax system in 2025.[7] This could well be due to the influence of the burgeoning Green party, who are strong supporters of LVT.

APPENDIX 2

CASE STUDY: THE NEW ZEALAND EXPERIENCE

LVT—Found and Lost: Why was a successful system of LVT abandoned?

~

This account of New Zealand's experience of LVT is an abbreviation of the full version, which may be found on my website: http://landvaluetaxguide.com/category/related-essays/

~

New Zealand holds a rather special status in that it was notably the first country to introduce a system of LVT for raising revenue.[1]

As part of the process of empire building at the end of the 18th century, Britain laid claim to the territory of New Zealand, which was considered to be an extension of the Australian colony of New South Wales. In the early 1800s the first colonists from England were Christian missionaries, followed by settlers, some 20 years after the first arrivals at Botany Bay in Australia.

The number of settlers increased rapidly and led to disputes with the native Maori, especially over land.

The Maori wars with the British arose basically out of disputes over land ownership and encroaching European occupation. In 1840 the Treaty of Waitangi was agreed with the Maori, who were acknowledged as owners of the land of New Zealand.

However, in England, in 1846, the Secretary of State for the Colonies, who had been unhappy with the terms of the treaty, issued instructions to lay claim to all the land not directly occupied by the Maori. But the new Governor, Sir George Grey, believing that this would alienate the Maori, devised a scheme whereby the land, rather than being appropriated, would be purchased piecemeal, albeit for paltry prices.

In order to raise local revenue, taxes were applied to property in imitation of the rates system in Britain where the building and the site were valued in combination. But it would seem that under the Grey administration certain progressive ideas about taxing only the land were brought from Britain.

As early as 1849, in Wellington and Marlborough provinces, legislation was proposed allowing for rates to be imposed on the value of land only—excluding improvements.[2] This was some 30 years before Henry George published *Progress and Poverty*. However, there is no record of any legislation having been acted upon.

The first evidence of actual implementation was in the town of New Plymouth, in 1855. In that legislation it was decreed that, if the ratepayers so decided, the rate could be on unimproved land value only.[3]

This was a clear demonstration of local democracy in action, which established a precedent that was to endure at the local level as a principle for the next 130 years. This local taxation system was adopted generally and continued up to the Rating Act of 1876, when modifications were introduced.

It is worth noting the prominent role played by Governor Grey in promoting LVT for New Zealand. He was the Governor General from 1845 to 1853, and later Premier from 1877 to 1879, both periods in which important advances were made for LVT. Grey was a progressive liberal and would have been familiar with the new reformist ideas being discussed in the early 19th century. David Ricardo had published his *Principles of Political Economy and Taxation* in 1817 and expounded his theory of the 'economic rent', an idea that Grey no doubt took with him to New Zealand.

It is known that prior to his term in office as Premier he met up with John Stuart Mill, another advocate of land value taxation.[4] Also, in 1871, Henry George published *Our Land and Land Policy* and, in 1890, made a lecture tour of Australia and New Zealand.

Central government revenue in the early years was mainly derived from customs and excise duties and the sale and leasing of land, appropriated or bought from the Maori.[5] But as the government started to run out of land to sell, by the 1870s it turned to property taxes, and introduced the Rating Act of 1876. This marked the beginning of national property taxation. But again, it was the British combined rating system that was generally adopted.

Attempts to introduce a national property tax based only on land values was a protracted affair, which began in 1878 with the Land Tax Act, introduced when Grey was Premier. In 1879 his finance minister John Balance, also an advocate of LVT, introduced a General Property Tax based on the selling value of land, but this was soon repealed by the succeeding National (conservative) government. Attempts to introduce a full land value tax at national level were often thwarted by opposition within the government itself, which as in England had many representatives of land-owning interests. Rolland O'Regan, in his book *Rating in New Zealand*, describes the slow progress:

> In 1894 the Rating on Unimproved Value Bill was introduced as a policy measure. It was passed by the House but rejected by the Legislative Council. The same process was repeated again in 1895. In this year it was carried by an overwhelming majority in the House and defeated by one vote in the Legislative Council. In 1896 the same bill again passed the House. This time the Council withdrew its opposition and it became law.[6]

A further attempt to use land value only for all rates was tried in 1901 but was abandoned due to opposition in the government's own ranks.[7] It was not until 1912 that the Rating Amendment Act was passed allowing for a full tax on land values on all rates. From this point it could be said that New Zealand had complete land value tax systems in place at local and national levels. The 1912 act continued in force until 1967 when, under a national administration, the local tax on land value was applied again to only certain rates—a retrogressive step. Perhaps this was the first move towards abolition, which was to culminate in the events of the mid-1980s.

At local and national levels, the rating systems evolved so that three options were provided for assessing valuations, subject to selection by ratepayer's poll:

- Combined land and improvements assessed by annual rental value. (AV)—the British system.
- Combined land and improvements assessed by capital value (CV).
- Unimproved land value only (LV).

At the local level, it is noteworthy that during the course of the 20th century, where there was freedom of choice, the ratepayers preferred the land value tax system (LV), so that by the 1980s the majority of local authorities employed this method. In an article on the history of rating in New Zealand, Robert Keall notes,

> By 1982 hundreds of rating polls had been held, so that in just 86 years 90% of all municipalities had by poll adopted land value rating, which accounted for 80% of local government revenue.[8]

The figures of Table 6 are taken from a paper by McCluskey and Franzsen, which show the number of boroughs using the different systems in the 55 years between 1942 and 1997.[9]

Year	AV	CV	LV	Duration
1942	8	37	55	—
1985	5	10	80	43 years
1997	2	30	64	12 years

Table 6. Different Local Tax Valuation Systems: 1942–97

In a general observation Keall states:

> Wherever Land Value Rating applies it has been adopted by poll of ratepayers, representing a lot of work and profound social concern. Wherever Capital or Annual Value Rating applies it has been imposed by Government or Councils, contrary to the express wishes of the ratepayers in almost every case.[10]

With certain exceptions[11] local LVT, assessed through the LV system, was preferred where democratic choice was allowed, but in 1988 this choice was removed, ironically by a Labour government, which revoked the democratic polls that had kept the local LVT in place for more than 130 years.

The history of the national land value tax took a rather different turn. Initially it was successful in raising revenue, but perhaps less so than the new income tax, which was gaining in popularity with most governments throughout the world. The land value tax continued well into the next century but from the 1920s went into decline almost as a matter of government policy. On the national tax, Keall comments,

> By 1922, the land tax yielded about 10% of the budget. As overseas trade developed and inflation became the accepted means of financing wars or social policy, so land values grew and were protected from any land tax by governments elected to do just that at all costs. Thus by 1989, or 98 years after its confirmation, the land tax yielded only 0.4 percent of the budget and was commonly regarded as an antiquated irritant.[12]

In the course of the 20th century, New Zealand followed the pattern of other western capitalist systems being in thrall to, if not in league with, the rich and powerful, who were often landed property owners. These vested interests played a large part in the inexorable decline of the national land value tax in New Zealand. After the optimism of the 'Georgist' period prior to World War One, vested interests prevailed and, mainly through exemptions and under-valuations, the national tax was enfeebled and rendered insignificant in terms of revenue collected.

A significant event, contributing to the decline of the tax was a provision in the 1976 Land Tax Act in which principal residences were exempted. This of course reduced the tax base and seriously undermined the effectiveness of the tax. But perhaps the main reason for the decline was the attitude of successive governments which were indifferent or even hostile to the land value tax, preferring instead to raise revenue through income and sales taxes.

By contrast, in the hands of local ratepayers, the local land value tax, fared much better, but even this was brought to an abrupt end in the rather dramatic events of the 1980s.

So what happened at that time?

After World War Two, the sequence of political events in New Zealand were very similar to those of Britain; the see-sawing of political control between two opposing main parties, one of the right (National) and the other of the left (Labour).

By 1984 the National party of Robert Muldoon had been in power for nine years and the economy was in crisis. A new Labour government under David Lange came to power in July 1984 with the express purpose of rescuing the situation, and the prime player in this operation was Lange's finance minister, Roger Douglas, who was to become instrumental in the demise of LVT. Douglas, supposedly on the left of the political spectrum, and ironically, a former member of the New Zealand Land Value Rating Association,[13] introduced a series of right-wing policies in his radical solution to the crisis. Contrary to his previous Labour background, he introduced a series of measures, which were straight from the neoliberal school of thought prevailing at the time (see Appendix 1). An account by the journalist Simon Louisson of the New Zealand Press Association records:

> The United States was in the grip of Ronald Reagan's free market Reaganomics while Margaret Thatcher was also pursuing Chicago School of Economics' monetarist policies. But neither went as far as New Zealand under Finance Minister Roger Douglas...[14]

An article on the website New Zealand History.net describes the events in 1986:

> Radical change came thick and fast: deregulation, privatisation, the sale of state assets, and the removal of subsidies, tariffs and price controls.[15]

Among these reforms the continuation of LVT stood little chance. The national LVT had already become insignificant in terms of revenue and was abolished in 1991. Robert Keall comments,

> The tax had become a political football. So, to pre-empt a National opposition promise to abolish the tax, the Labour government did just that.[16]

On the local rates he notes,

> Since the time of restructuring in 1989, combining urban with rural areas, the 90% of municipalities which by poll had adopted land value rating has been reduced to about 40%.[17]

And also,

> In the Rating Powers Act of 1988–89 the government withdrew the traditional right to demand a poll.[18]

Henceforth, it became the local authorities rather than the people that decided which form of rates to adopt. Between 1989 and 1999 many local authorities, which were in high value urban areas, switched from LV to CV, to the advantage of wealthier residents.[19] The local rates, based on unimproved value (LV), which had always depended on the popular polls for their continuance, suffered a great set back when the government revoked this democratic process in 1988.[20] Thus, in New Zealand, within a few years in the 1980s, 95 years of national LVT was lost and 133 years of local LVT severely diminished.

The question still remains. Why did New Zealand lose its grip on LVT?

For a great number of years, it seemed to be very well established, at least at the local level. From the foregoing account it would appear that in the case of the national tax, it was largely a matter of central government indifference or neglect, even downright hostility. In the case of the local tax, in the final years it appeared to be more a matter of overt ideological government opposition. The national tax was allowed to die slowly over a long period, whereas the local rates, after a long period in the ascendant, went into abrupt decline from 1985 onwards. In both cases the opposition to LVT stemmed from the governing authorities, not from the people. In a paper on land taxation in New Zealand Barret and Veal make the comment that, 'To a great extent successive governments allowed the tax to fail.'[21]

After World War Two the revenue from the national land tax continued to decline, so that by 1967 a government taxation review committee recommended its abolition. Perhaps this review signified the beginning of the end for the national land tax. In 1982 another government report noted that the land tax had 'no perceptible redistributive effect' and was 'not an adequate indicator of the taxable capacity provided by wealth.'[22] And so it would seem that government opposition to the land value tax was already under way before the later events initiated by Roger Douglas.

In the 1970s and 80s the neoclassical school of thinking dominated world economics, including the central banks, the IMF, the World Bank and the universities. This was the period that saw the rise of 'Reaganomics' in the Reagan–Thatcher era hallmarked by deregulation, privatisation and the dominance of neoliberalism. It was at the height of this world movement in 1984 that the new Labour government came to power in New Zealand and under the finance minister Douglas, carried out its drastic right-wing policies.

For those on the right, Douglas was the hero that rescued New Zealand from the crisis, but for those on the left the words of former prime minister Lange are perhaps more significant: In 1996, relenting on the effects of Douglas' policies he is recorded as saying,

> For people who don't want the government in their lives this has been a bonanza. For people who are disabled, limited, resourceless, uneducated, this has been a tragedy.[23]

Land value taxation, at least at the local level, was an undeniable success in New Zealand. It was tried and tested over a long period of time, but as with freedom itself, as the old adage goes, it is only appreciated when lost. For LVT enthusiasts there are clearly lessons to be learnt from the New Zealand experience.

APPENDIX 3

CASE STUDY: THE PITTSBURGH EXPERIENCE

LVT – Found and Lost: Why was a successful system of LVT abandoned?

~

This account of the Pittsburgh split-rate tax is an abbreviation of the full version, which may be found on my website: http://landvaluetaxguide.com/category/related-essays/

~

LVT operated as a local tax in Pittsburgh from 1914 to 2001. It was a split-rate property tax where the site and the building upon it were taxed at different rates. At the beginning of the period the ratio was set at 2:1, where the portion due to the site value paid two thirds of the total and that due to the building value one third. In later years the ratio was increased to as much as 6:1. In Pittsburgh itself the tax was known as the Graded Tax, due to the gradual method of its introduction—over a ten-year period. It was introduced when the Georgist movement was at its height of popularity and Georgist principles were well understood by the politicians in power. Its demise 87 years later was not due to any lack of success in raising revenue, or any particular opposition from the taxpayers, but by the gradual undermining of its effectiveness due to a faulty valuation system.

From 1914 to 1942 the valuations were made at three-yearly intervals by the city assessors, and the tax was administered without difficulty. The valuations for the other local taxes, school districts, utility districts and other county taxes, were the separate responsibility of the county assessors.

The graded tax did not provoke any untoward public protest or opposition during this period. But in the late 1930s, in order to avoid duplication of effort, the proposition was made that all valuations should be done only by the county assessors. The city assessors, who were generally in favour of the split rate, resisted being taken over, but after some years of argument, the county assessors, who were generally against the split rate, prevailed and the change was made in 1942.

Thereafter things were never quite the same. Over the years the integrity of the valuation/assessment system was constantly eroded by ever increasing periods between valuations and reliance on the 'base year' system, whereby new assessments were based on an earlier assessment, without a new revaluation taking place.

It was also undermined by the constant interference of politicians promising voters to reduce taxes and putting pressure on assessors to make under-valuations. Eventually when, in 1998, an attempt was made to carry out realistic assessments, the accumulated disparities were so great that the taxpayers protested en masse. They unfairly blamed the split-rate tax and within three years, after much debate and argument, the tax was rescinded. But this sad story is belied by the clear success of the split-rate tax when it was able to function properly, especially in the earlier years.

The tax operated with undoubted success for the first 28 years and provided Pittsburgh with a stable property tax that saw it through the depredations of the 1930s.

The LVT advocate Dan Sullivan cites the fall in land prices, between 1930 and 1940, of several comparable cities: 'Detroit 58%, Cleveland 46%, Boston 28%, New Orleans 27%, Cincinnati 26%, Milwaukee 25%, New York 21% and Pittsburgh 11%.'[1]

These figures speak for themselves. The existence of the higher tax on land in Pittsburgh had constrained the escalation of prices that had taken place elsewhere in the 1920s. The split-rate tax had 'discouraged speculators from bidding up prices during the previous boom.'[2] Up to the advent of World War Two the split-rate tax enjoyed much support at the level of local government. Thereafter, this advantage diminished as the years progressed and over time the basic Georgist ideas became largely forgotten, except by the ardent supporters. By the end of the century the split-rate tax was seen by the general public as 'just another tax'.

The early success of the split-rate tax was undoubtedly tempered by the concurrent introduction of the income tax in 1913, which became a competing factor for the attention of politicians constantly seeking ways of raising revenue. Although the initial application was at the national level, the income tax grew in influence at all levels of government, federal, state and local, becoming eventually the dominant tax, not only in the US but throughout the world. But it also had the effect of undermining the Georgist movement from the start.

At a Council for Georgist Organisations conference in 2013, Alex Wagner Lough suggested that the 'Passage of the income tax marks the decline of the Georgist movement and might have caused it.'[3] It certainly caused a schism in the Georgist ranks— Henry George was always opposed to it. But despite his formidable powers of persuasion in promoting the land value tax throughout the world, his arguments did not, in later years, dissuade his own son from supporting the Income Tax bill through Congress. Dan Sullivan notes,

> Wilson's administration, awash with Georgist leaders, proposed the 1913 income tax, and Congressman Henry George Jr. co-sponsored the legislation.[4]

This schism did not help the Georgist cause, but nevertheless legislation for the graded tax survived the difficulty.

Another negative influence that has to be mentioned was the neoclassical movement in economics that dominated academic thought throughout the period. The neoclassical economists saw land as just another form of capital and were generally opposed to the idea of land value taxation (see Appendix 1). They were always in the background and ready to give support to any manifestations of opposition to the split-rate tax.

In the *Pacific Standard News* website of October 2009, a pro-LVT contributor, in a discussion of Henry George, noted, 'He's been out of favour for decades, especially in graduate schools. Economists are trained to ignore him.'[5]

Nevertheless, in the earlier years, the obvious benefits of the split-rate property tax continued to be recognised and appreciated as much for its results as for its Georgist principles. Sullivan records that, as early as May 1915, the *Pittsburgh Press* reported, 'The law is working to the complete satisfaction of everybody except a few real estate speculators who hope to hold idle land until its value is greatly increased by improvements erected on surrounding territory.'[6] In a 1955 essay on Pennsylvania, former city chief city assessor, Percy Williams, records a comment in the *Pittsburgh Post* of 1927:

> Formerly land held vacant here was touched lightly by taxation, even as it was being greatly enhanced in value by building around it, the builders being forced to pay the chief toll, almost as though being fined for adding to the wealth of the community. Now the builders in Pittsburgh are encouraged; improvements are taxed just one half the rate levied upon vacant land. Building has increased accordingly.[7]

In an address to an LVT Conference in London in 1936, Dr John C. Rose also claimed that the split-rate tax stabilised Pittsburgh's municipal credit; 'A stabilised credit is a wonderful asset to any city or community.'[8]

On the issue of land speculation; in a 1963 paper, Williams claimed: 'Land speculation is no longer a major factor in Pittsburgh.'[9] He goes on to list a whole range of 27 well-known national magazines that had published favourable articles between 1946 and 1960.[10] Sullivan adds: 'Every one of the 19 land-taxing cities in Pennsylvania enjoyed a construction surge after shifting to LVT, even though their nearest neighbours continued to decline.'[11] In a definitive 1996 academic study Oates and Schwab suggested that 'The Pittsburgh tax reform, properly understood, has played a significant supportive role in the economic resurgence of the city.'[12]

Although most of the examples of Pittsburgh's success are related to the revival of the central business district and other downtown areas, there was also a beneficial effect on out-of-town residential areas where site values were lower. Williams makes the important point:

> It is the homeowner who emerges as the chief beneficiary of the graded tax. This is widely recognised as one of the principal reasons why this plan has popular support. Only in rare instances do we find a homeowner paying a higher tax under the graded tax. The typical homeowner's investment is largely in building rather than land, it being quite common for the assessed value of the house to be as much as five times the value of the site, and often this ratio is exceeded.[13]

Perhaps the high point was in 1998 when, at federal level, legislation by the Senate and the House passed to allow the two-rate system for nearly 1,000 boroughs in Pennsylvania. But despite this apparent confirmation of success, within three years the Pittsburgh split-rate system would be rescinded.

So what went wrong? How can one account for this sudden reversal of fortune. Mark Alan Hughes makes the cautionary comment,

> The 2001 abandonment of the split-rate in Pittsburgh is a compelling example of the limited role that evidence often plays in policy decisions.[14]

As with many economic changes the causes often have a long gestation period, and I suggest this was the case with the split-rate tax in Pittsburgh. Perhaps the turning point in its fortunes began in 1942 when the responsibility for carrying out valuations changed hands.

After the boom years of World War Two all the north-east states were hit by a decline in heavy industry which eventually gave rise to the so-called 'rust belt'. With its vulnerable steel industry Pittsburgh was at the centre of this decline. However, thanks to its split-rate tax policy it survived better than other comparable cities. This did not pass unnoticed: In 1960 House and Home, the construction industry's leading trade journal quoted the Pennsylvania Governor and former mayor of Pittsburgh from 1946 to 1959, David Lawrence, as saying:

> There is no doubt in my mind that the graded-tax law has been a good thing for the city of Pittsburgh. It has discouraged the holding of vacant land for speculation and provided an incentive for building improvements. It produced a more prosperous city.[15]

Whereas many old industrial cities struggled to halt the decline in their fortunes, Pittsburgh became known throughout the US as a city that had best been able to cope with the problems, demonstrated by its continuing building activity and avoidance of dereliction, especially in the central city areas. Walter Rybeck notes that, 'Pittsburgh thrived with its two-to-one land-building ratio. After World War Two, despite the decline of its steel industry, Pittsburgh enjoyed a renaissance.'[16] Perhaps for this reason enthusiasm for the split-rate idea continued in Pennsylvania.

In 1951 the State legislated to allow for the split rate to be adopted by 3rd class cities* and at the same time abolished the limit on the 2:1 ratio. These options were taken up by Harrisburg, in 1975, McKeesport, Newcastle, Duquesne, Washington, Aliquippa, Clairton and Oil City in the 1980s, Titusville in 1990, Coatsville, Du Bois, Hazleton and Lock Haven in 1991 and Allentown in 1996.[17]

In Pittsburgh, the split-rate tax was recognised as helpful in re-vitalising the city and in 1978–80 the land to building tax ratio was increased from 2:1 to 5:1— with beneficial results. The change of ratio increased the penalty on land holders for keeping land out of use and stimulated a further building boom, the results of which are well documented in a study by Oates and Schwab (see Table 7). The study compares the relative situations of 15 'rust belt' cities in the period 20 years before and ten years after 1979, as measured by the value

---

* In the US, cities are classified according to the size of population.

of building permits. The value of building permits issued is taken as a measure of new building activity and therefore the prosperity of a community.

	1960–79	1980–89	% Change
Akron	134,026	87,907	– 34.41
Allentown	48,124	28,801	– 40.15
Buffalo	93,749	82,930	– 11.54
Canton	40,235	24,251	– 39.73
Cincinnati	318,248	231,561	– 27.24
Cleveland	329,511	224,587	– 31.84
Columbus	456,580	527,026	15.43
Dayton	107,798	92,249	– 14.42
Detroit	368,894	277,783	– 24.70
Erie	48,353	22,761	– 52.93
Pittsburgh	181,734	309,727	70.43
Rochester	118,726	82,411	– 30.59
Syracuse	94,503	53,673	– 43.21
Toledo	138,384	93,495	– 32.44
Youngstown	33,688	11,120	– 66.99
15 city average	167,504	143,352	– 14.42

Table 7. Comparative list of average annual values of building permits.

NB: All figures are in thousands of US dollars at 1982 values

(Source: Table 3 of paper by Wallace E. Oates and Robert M. Schwab: 'The impact of Urban Land Taxation: The Pittsburgh Experience, JSTOR *National Tax Journal*, vol. 50,no.1,1997, pp. 1–21. www.jstor.org/stable/41789240)

The results revealed that only Pittsburgh showed a large increase. Columbus, Ohio, also showed an increase, but Oates and Schwab suggest this may have been due to annexations of surrounding jurisdictions, that took place during the same period. The value of permits showed an average decline for all 15 cities of 14.42%, but a 70.43% increase for Pittsburgh (a 15.43% increase for Columbus).

However, despite its obvious success, support for the graded tax was beginning to weaken. Hughes notes that, 'By the late 1970s the consensus began to fracture.'[18] But the main reason for the abandonment of the graded tax was the faulty system of assessments, which had become increasingly more dysfunctional in the decades prior to 2001. Hughes notes that in 1979, 'The assessments of both land and building values remained essentially fixed in this period, and indeed for the next twenty years.'[19]

Another major influence that worked against the split-rate tax throughout the whole period was the neoclassical view of economics, which gained in popularity amongst economists as the years passed, and which was also in the interests of the large landholders. Also, the income tax—the wage tax at the local level—was often preferred by politicians for raising revenue.

The demise of the split-rate tax occurred suddenly in the last few years, precipitated by a bungled revaluation, which was begun in 1998 and carried out by Sabre Systems, a private company. The intention was to bring the assessments up to date after so many years of neglect, but the way it was handled was a disaster. Sabre Systems were occupied for over two years with this major operation, which involved an initial report in 2000, followed by a second report in 2001.

The first preliminary report contained a combined assessment that anticipated that the land value share would be approximately 20% of the total. But this initial assessment did not reveal the previously gross under-assessments of the land factor. However, it was made public and led the taxpayers to believe that the proposed future increases would be reasonable. When the final assessment notices were issued in 2001, showing separate valuations, the land element was much higher than had been previously indicated. Between the two reports the assessments for land value had effectively increased by 81%, and for building value by 43%.[20] These higher-than-expected tax demands caused much confusion and resentment and led to the eventual rescission.

In a 2010 article on the Philly Record website, Steven Cord, a previous member of the city council recalls that:

> Well-to-do voters in Pittsburgh were suddenly aroused to fever pitch about their property tax as never before because a county re- assessment increased their land assessments from five to eight times overnight.[21]

Bill Bradley writing on the Next City website in August 2013 noted one of the actions that brought the graded tax to an end,

> The city's unique tax structure was ended, as wealthy homeowners outmanoeuvred downtown developers and poorer residents to strike it down.[22]

Hughes summarised the situation in saying,

> The existence of the split rate made a bad problem
> worse and was processed as the cause rather than
> just a magnification.[23]

The confusion over the property tax assessments
continued after 2001, and to this day remains basically
unresolved. Ironically, the elimination of the split-rate
tax, the supposed cause of the problem, made no
difference to the ongoing crisis. In his '238 report'
Steven Cord records:

> After it rescinded its land tax, Pittsburgh suffered
> a 19.5% decline (adjusted for inflation) in private
> new construction in the three years after rescission
> as compared to the three years before.[24]

Also,

> A computer examination of the entire Pittsburgh
> assessment roll found that 54% of all homeowners
> paid more property tax after the rescission.[25]

The final Sabre assessments gave rise to more than
90,000 appeals. Further assessments carried out in 2002
showed an average tax increase of 11%, leading to
another 90,000 appeals.[26]

As with the New Zealand experience, described in
Appendix 2, there are also lessons to be learnt from the
Pittsburgh story.

NOTES

Introduction

1. Adam Smith, *The Wealth of Nations*, 1776. Current publication for reference purposes: Penguin Classics, 1999, edited by Andrew Skinner, book 5, chapter 2, pp. 493–494.
2. Henry George, *Progress and Poverty*, 1879, Cosimo Classics, New York, 2005.
3. Smith, *The Wealth of Nations*, book 5, chapter 2, pp. 416–417: In later years these four maxims were supplemented, through the work of other economists, with the additional maxims (or canons) of Productivity, Elasticity, Simplicity and Diversity. Refer to Economics Concepts.com https://economicsconcepts.com/canons_of_taxation.htm
4. The origin of the statement is credited to the English playwright Christopher Bullock, author of *The Cobbler of Preston* (1716).
   https://www.adamsmith.org/blog/death-and-taxes
5. Oliver Bullough, *Moneyland*, Profile books, London, 2018, p. 21.
6. http://www.ramsdale.org/hearth.htm
7. 'Land for the Many', Report for the Labour Party, June 2019. https://labour.org.uk/wp-content/uploads/2019/06/12081_19-Land-for-the-Many.pdf
8. Will Hutton, *The State We're In*, Jonathan Cape Ltd, 1995, p. 304.
9. Robert V. Andelson (editor), *Land Value Taxation Around the World*, 2000, Blackwell Publishers, p. xxxiii.

10. Mark Braund, *The Possibility of Progress*, Shepheard-Walwyn, 2005, p. 108.
11. https://patrioticmillionaires.org/
12. https://www.theguardian.com/news/2021/oct/25/millionaires-petition-rishi-sunak-to-introduce-wealth-tax
13. School of Cooperative Individualism, Henry George and his Principles https://www.cooperative-individualism.org/einstein-albert_henry-george-and-his-principles-1934.htm

Chapter 1: Basic Principles

1. Smith, *The Wealth of Nations,* book 5, chapter 2, pp. 492–493.

Chapter 2: Economic Evolution

1. For an excellent example of contemporary infrastructure co-operation refer to video, 'The Bridge at Qeswachaka': https://kottke.org/15/07/the-bridge-at-qeswachaka
2. Sparknotes, US history, Land Policy and Speculation, summary, p. 2, para. 1. http://www.sparknotes.com/history/american/westwardexpansion/section2.rhtml
3. Ibid. p. 1, para. 1.

Chapter 3: Application and Advantages

1. Current UK eco-taxes are, fuel duties, climate change levy, air passenger duty, vehicle excise duties and landfill tax. Sin taxes are alcohol duties, tobacco duties and betting and gaming duties.
2. Refer to Josh Vincent, *Strong Towns* website. https://www.strongtowns.org/journal/2019/3/6/non-glamorous-gains-the-pennsylvania-land-tax-experiment
3. In Australia, in 2012, the Australian Capital Territories (Canberra) introduced LVT to replace Stamp Duty over a 20-year period.

https://thenewdaily.com.au/money/property/2019/04/05/land-tax-stamp-duty-debate/

4. Walter Rybeck. Chapter 9 of *Land Value Taxation Around the World*, third edition, 2000, Blackwell Publishers, edited by Robert V. Andelson p. 169.

5. Institute for Government: 'Local government funding in England' item 2. https://www.instituteforgovernment.org.uk/explainers/local- government-funding-england

6. Rolland O'Regan, *Rating in New Zealand*, 1973, Baranduin. Publishers Ltd. Waiuiomata, New Zealand, p. 179.

7. Institute for Government, "Local government...' item 3.

8. Tony Vickers, *Location Matters*, Shepheard-Walwyn Ltd. 2007, p. 58.

Chapter 4: History

1. National Archives talk by Mark Pearsal: http://www.nationalarchives.gov.uk/documents/land-tax.mp3

2. https://liberalhistory.org.uk/history/the-newcastle-programme/

3. Refer LVT supporters listed on: http://landvaluetaxguide.com/category/supporters/

4. Owen Connellan, *Land Value Taxation in Britain*, Lincoln Institute of Land Policy, Cambridge Massachusetts, 2004, chapter 5, pp. 52–53.

5. Brett Christophers, *The New Enclosure*, Verso Books, 2019, p. 110.

6. Winston Churchill, *The People's Rights*, 1909, Jonathan Cape, London, p. 123.

7. https://www.lincolninst.edu/publications/articles/tax-increment- financing

8. https://www.libdemvoice.org/liblink-tim-leunig-land-auctions-will- help-give-us-the-homes-we-need-23450.html

9. https://publications.parliament.uk/pa/cm201719/cmselect/cmcomloc/7 66/766.pdf

Chapter 5: Aspects of LVT

1. Smith, *The Wealth of Nations,* Book 5, chap. 2, p. 433.
2. Paul Collier, *The Future of Capitalism,* Penguin Random House, 2018, p. 134.
3. Using figures from the Valuation Office Agency: *Property Market Report 2011*, and an article by Thomas Aubrey, 'Gathering the Windfall', Centre for Progressive policy, 19 September 2018. https://www.progressive-policy.net/publications/gathering-the-windfall-how-changing-land-law-can-unlock-englands-housing- supply-potential
4. http://www.ft.com/intl/cms/s/2/5a4c57ea-1612-11e3-a57d-00144feabdc0.html#axzz2raqku0bC
5. Mark Braund, *The Possibility of Progress*, Shepheard-Walwyn Ltd., 2005, p. 222
6. Andrew MacLaren (1883-1975): Independent Labour MP for Burslem (1922-45), LVT advocate and educator.
7. David Bollier, *Silent Theft*, Routledge, New York, 2003, p. 60.
8. Robert D. Keall. Chapter 26 of *Land Value Taxation Around the World*, third edition, 2000, Blackwell Publishers, edited by Robert V. Andelson, p. 436.
9. Andy Wightman, *The Poor Had no Lawyers*, Birlinn Ltd., Edinburgh, 2013, p. 95.
10. ibid. p. 2.
11. ibid. p. 340.
12. George, *Progress and Poverty,* p. 259.
13. In an interesting chapter in his book, Collier refers to the respected economist Willem Buiter's scathing comment that one third of lawyers 'are socially predatory: they are employed in the legal scams that fleece the productive. They

are the ultimate rent-seekers': Collier, *The Future of Capitalism,* p. 186.

14. George, *Progress and Poverty,* p. 260.
15. ibid. pp. 287-288.
16. John Locke, *Second Treatise of Civil Government,*1689, para. 27, Chapter https://www.marxists.org/reference/subject/politics/locke/ch05.htm Also, refer to the essay by George H Smith: John Locke, 'The Justification of Private Property.' https://www.libertarianism.org/columns/john-locke-justification- private-property
17. The Ostrom rebuttal of Hardin is well described in an article by the environmentalist and science journalist Michelle Nijhuis: https://aeon.co/essays/the-tragedy-of-the-commons-is-a-false-and-dangerous-myth
18. Guardian article by Fiona Harvey, 10.7.13. 'Fishing quotas can be re-distributed to favour smaller vessels.' https://www.theguardian.com/environment/2013/jul/10/fishing-quotas-smaller-vessels-court
19. Guardian Agencies article, 5.1.19. https://www.theguardian.com/world/2019/jan/05/sushi-king-pays-record-31m-for-endangered-bluefin-tuna-in-japan
20. United Nations FAO fisheries technical paper 467: Rome, 2004. http://www.fao.org/3/y5428e/y5428e03.htm
21. Churchill, *The People's Rights* p. 125.
22. Andrew Purves, *No Debt, High Growth, Low Tax: Hong Kong's Economic Miracle Explained'*, Shepheard-Walwyn Ltd., London, 2015.
23. https://www.heritage.org/index/ranking
24. Comprehensively discussed in *The Stewardship Economy,* by Julian Pratt. Lulu.com, Creative commons, San Francisco, USA. 2011.
25. Fred Harrison et al., *The Corruption of Economics,* 1994, Shepheard-Walwyn Ltd. p. 223
26. Julian Pratt, *The Stewardship Economy,* p. 22.

Chapter 6: Land Values

1. Duncan Pickard, *Lie of the Land*, Land Research Trust & Shepheard- Walwyn, London, 2005, p. 41.

2. https://www.gov.uk/government/uploads/system/uploads/attachment_ data/file/371470/pmr_2011.pdf

3. http://pdf.euro.savills.co.uk/uk/rural-other/uk-agricultural-land- 2016.pdf

4. http://demonstrations.wolfram.com/LocationTheoryLand UseDetermi nation/

5. http://www.thisismoney.co.uk/money/mortgageshome/article- 1619589/Record-959m-for-barracks-building-site.html

6. http://www.uklanddirectory.org.uk/building-land-plot-sales- london.asp

7. Pratt, *The Stewardship Economy*, p. 66.

8. http://capreform.eu/farmers-share-of-food-chain-value-added/

9. https://uk.jobted.com/salary

10. www.gov.uk/government/statistics/familyfood

11. https://www.statista.com/statistics/284881/clothing-share-of-household-spending

12. https://www.ov0energy.com/guides/energy-guides/how-much-heating-energy-do-you-think-you-use

13. https://www.statista.com/statistics/755883/income-spent-on-mortgage-or-rent-england

14. https://www.which.co.uk/news/2019/11/heres-how-our-food-prices-compare-to-30-years-ago-and-you-might-be-surprised/

15. https://fareshare.org.uk/what-we-do/hunger-food-waste/

16. Collins and Larragy, 'A Site Value Tax for Ireland' p. 2, Introduction https://www.researchgate.net/publication/241767601_A_Site_Value Tax_for_Ireland_Approach_Design_and_Implementation

Chapter 7: Housing

1. Josh Ryan-Collins, Toby Lloyd & Laurie Macfarlane, *Rethinking the Economics of Land and Housing*, Zed Books Ltd. 2017, p. 147.
2. Garry B. Nixon. Chapter 4 of *Land Value Taxation Around the World*, third edition, 2000, Blackwell Publishers, edited by Robert V. Andelson, p. 67.
3. https://www.strongtowns.org/journal/2019/3/6/non-glamorous-gains- the-pennsylvania-land-tax-experiment
4. https://www.examinerlive.co.uk/news/west-yorkshire-news/kirklees- council-tax-three-times-16021996
5. http://www.bexley-is- bonkers.co.uk/local_taxes/league_table/2019.php
6. Ryan-Collins et al., *Rethinking the Economics...* p. 14.
7. This rule still holds true despite the fact of land reclamation—of which the Dutch have a vast experience over centuries—but the reclaimed land in the Netherlands is mostly of only rural value. The culverting of rivers, such as the Wallbrook and Fleet in London was an early form of 'making' land, but it has long since been absorbed into the overall pattern and does not alter the general rule of fixed supply.
   Refer to: https://www.thoughtco.com/polders-and-dikes-of-the- netherlands-1435535
8. Christophers, *The New Enclosure*. pp. 102-103.
9. Ryan-Collins et al., *Rethinking the Economics...* p. 173.
10. Bob Colenutt, *The Property lobby*, Policy Press, Bristol, 2020, pp. 92–93.
11. Refer to: http://housescheaperbettermore.blogspot.fr/2017/07/buildingmore- houses-wont-bring-down.html
12. See Josh Ryan-Collins UCL IIPP article of 26. 2. 20, 'When it comes to high house prices, it's not enough to just blame low interest rates. https://medium.com/iipp-blog/when-it-comes-to-high-house-prices- its-not-enough-to-just-blame-low-interest-rates-here-s-why- c0d91e63b253

13. Josh Ryan-Collins, *Why Can't You Afford a Home?* Polity Press, Cambridge, UK, 2019, p. 68

14. Ryan-Collins, UCL IIPP article, 'When it comes...' p. 5.

15. Christopher Walker, Council of Mortgage Lenders, Research. 2016
https://thinkhouse.org.uk/site/assets/files/1840/cml.pdf

16. Source: Bank of England data, British Landlords Association: https://thebla.co.uk/uk-interest-rate-history-base-rate-graph/

17. CPRE Brownfield Report, 2019. https://www.cpre.org.uk/resources/housing-and- planning/planning/item/5086-state-of-brownfield-2019

18. Christophers, *The New Enclosure,* p. 300.

19. Thomas Aubrey on Housing: https://www.progressive-policy.net/publications/gathering-the-windfall-how-changing-land-law-can-unlock-englands-housing-supply-potential

20. Oliver Wainwright, 'Britain has enough land to solve the housing crisis' https://www.theguardian.com/cities/2017/jan/31/britain-land- housing-crisis-developers-not-building-land-banking

21. Paul Miner, 'The Scandal of Land Banking' https://westlancashirerecord.com/2018/12/12/the-scandal-of-land-banking-exposed-by-cpre/

22. Christophers, *The New Enclosure*, p. 246.

23. https://www.rte.ie/news/analysis-and-comment/2019/0118/1024157-vacant-site-levy/

24. An enquiry on this issue in 2018 led by the Conservative MP Oliver Letwin, recommended 'to cap the value of land at 10 times the agricultural value'. https://www.local.gov.uk/sites/default/files/documents/Independent%20review%20of%20build%20out%20%20LGA%20briefing%20FINAL.pdf

Chapter 8: Other Economic Rent Collection Practices

1. Don Riley, *Taken for a Ride,* 2001, Centre for Land Policy Studies, Teddington UK.
   https://books.google.fr/books/about/Taken_for_a_Ride.
   html?id=rVZu mQEACAAJ&redir_esc=y
2. https://www.propertyreporter.co.uk/property/what-impact-are-the- crossrail-delays-having-on-house-price-grow.html
3. https://www.theguardian.com/artanddesign/2018/aug/14/the-line-that- ate-london-our-critics-verdict-on-the-15bn-crossrail-colossus- elizabeth-line
4. Ryan-Collins et al., *Rethinking the Economics...* p. 12.
5. Churchill, *The People's Rights,* p. 122.
6. Pickard, *Lie of the Land,* p. 44.

Chapter 9: Objections and Obstacles

1. The Mirrlees Review, Chapter 15, Taxes on Wealth Transfers. para. 1 https://www.ifs.org.uk/publications/5353
2. https://www.jstor.org/stable/2534911
3. http://www.wealthandwant.com/docs/Churchill_LPCP.html
4. http://www.wealthandwant.com/docs/unindexed/Batt_poor_widow_so lution.htm
5. http://www.city-data.com/forum/economics/2290999-big-lesson- small-nation.html
6. See paper by Anders Muller, p.11. http://www.and ywightman.com/docs/muller.pdf
7. http://www.landvaluetax.org/download-document/108-whitstable- 1964.html
8. http://www.andywightman.com/docs/LVTREPORT.pdf
9. http://www.labourland.org/downloads/papers/oxford shirelandvaluetax study.pdf
10. O'Regan, *Rating in New Zealand,* p. 82.

11. https://www.thetimes.co.uk/article/all-bidders-for-the-land-registry- have-links-to-tax-havens-q9vfqw029

12. Andrew Sayer, *Why We Can't Afford the Rich*, Policy Press, 2016, p. 239.

13. Collier, *The Future of Capitalism*, p. 86.

14. Rybeck/Andelson, *LVT Around the World*, p. 155.

15. Henry George Foundation, letter to Pope Leo X111 https://www.henrygeorgefoundation.org/the-science-of-economics/letter-to-pope-leo-xiii.html

16. Mason Gaffney, Dept. of Economics, University of California, *Henry* 'George, Dr. Edward McGlynn and Pope Leo X111' https://economics.ucr.edu/papers/papers01/01-02.pdf

17. Wightman, *The Poor Had No Lawyers,* p. 265.

18. Housing, Communities and Local Government Committee: "Land Value Capture. Tenth report of session, 2017-19'. https://publications.parliament.uk/pa/cm201719/cmselect/cmcomloc/ 766/766.pdf

19. Ibid. pp. 33-41.

20. 'LVT in Vancouver by Prof. C. England', 11.1.18. https://onlinelibrary.wiley.com/doi/full/10.1111/ajes.12218

21. Vickers, *Location Matters,* p. 28.

22. Collier, *The Future of Capitalism,* p. 136.

23. http://www.c4ej.com/appg

24. Antonia Swinson, *Root of All Evil,* St. Andrew Press, 2003, p. 66.

25. Chloe Kimberley, *Generation Rent,* Canbury Press, 2020, p. 270.

26. Ibid., p.271, also Fred Harrison, *As Evil Does,* Teddington: Geophilos, 2016, pp. 63–64.

27. Gaffney et al., *The Corruption of Economics,* p. 29 or visit link https://masongaffney.org/publications/K1Neo-classicalStratagem.CV.pdf

28. Refer to Land Value Tax Guide/supporters/individuals http://landvaluetaxguide.com/category/individuals/

29. Bollier, *Silent Theft*, p. 136.
30. Sayer, *Why We Can't Afford the Rich*, p. 349.

Chapter 10: Which Taxes?

1. George. *Progress and Poverty*, p. 268
2. Max Beer, *The Pioneers of land reform*. G. Bell and Sons Ltd.,1920, Introduction, p. V11, para. 2.
3. Prof. Mark A Lause, University of Cincinnati, paper: 'Progress Impoverished; Origin of Henry George's Single Tax', August 2007. p.398. https://www.researchgate.net/publication/229851153_Progress_Impov erished_Origin_of_Henry_George's_Single_Tax
4. Ibid. p. 395.
5. Edward J. Dodson, 'The Core of Economics and the Birth of American Labour', *Land and Liberty* magazine No.1247, Summer 2019. https://www.henrygeorgefoundation.org/publications/land- liberty-magazine.html
6. Dominic Frisby, *Daylight Robbery*, Penguin Business, UK, 2019. p. 151.
7. Ibid. p.174.
8. Forbes Rich List, 2020.
9. Frisby, *Daylight Robbery*, pp. 162
10. https://www.ukwealth.tax/
11. https://gala.gre.ac.uk/id/eprint/33819/20/33819%20 TIPPET_The_Cas e_for_a_Progressive_Annual_Wealth_Tax_%282021%29_v2.pdf
12. Refer to https://sites.google.com/site/justindkeith/home/geolibertarian-faq
13. Refer to: https://www.economist.com/schumpeter/2013/03/15/a- modest-proposal

Chapter 11: Welfare

1. Speenhamland: An Experiment in Guaranteed Income. Milton D. Speizman, *Chicago Journals* article, Social

Services Review, Vol 40, No. 1. https://www.journals.uchicago.edu/doi/abs/10.1086/641854?journalC%20ode=ssr&

2. Henry George, 'How to Help the Unemployed'. Article in The North American Review, February1894 pp. 175–184 http://www.wealthandwant.com/HG/how_to_help_the_unemployed.h tml

3. Drew Hendry MP, Left Foot Forward, article, 22nd January 2020, https://tinyurl.com/rfuwqp3

Chapter 13: Definitions

1. For more information on economic rents refer to: https://www.investopedia.com/terms/e/economicrent.asp

2. David Ricardo, *On The Principles of Political Economy and Taxation,* 1817 (third edition 1821), Batoche Books, Kitchener, 2001. p. 40. https://socialsciences.mcmaster.ca/econ/ugcm/3ll3/ricardo/Principles. pdf

3. Ibid, p. 42.

4. http://www.ethicaleconomics.org.uk/2016/06/the-law-of-rent-the- concept-2/

Appendix 1: Neoclassical Economics

1. George. *Progress and Poverty,* pp. 112–113.

2. Gaffney et al., *The Corruption of Economics*, p. 29.

3. William Batt, 'How the Railroads Got Us On The Wrong Economic Track', p. 4, para. 5. http://www.wealthandwant.com/docs/BattHTRGUOTWET.html

4. See video: https://www.youtube.com/watch?v=yS7Jb58hcsc

5. See Video: https://www.youtube.com/watch?v=j2mdYX1nF_Y

6. Refer to: Land Value Tax Guide–Supporters: http://landvaluetaxguide.com/category/individuals/

7. https://www.hgsss.org/event/land-value-tax-breakthrough-in-baden-wuerttemberg-germany/

Appendix 2: Case Study, The New Zealand Experience

1. Keall/Andelson, *Land Value Taxation...* p. 425.
2. O'Regan, *Rating...* p. 21, para.1.
3. Ibid. p. 21, para. 2.
4. Keall/Andelson, *Land Value Taxation...* p. 422, para. 5.
5. Te-ara Encyclopedia of New Zealand. Govt. revenue 1840–90. Graph. http://www.teara.govt.nz/en/graph/21529/government- revenue-1840-1890
6. O'Regan, *Rating...* p. 26, para. 2.
7. Ibid. p. 27. para. 2.
8. Robert D. Keall, 'A Short History of the N.Z. Land Value Rating Association.' Resource Rentals for Revenue, 2008. p.2,para.7.http://resourcerentalsrevenue.org/nz-association-short-history.html
9. McCluskey & Franzsen, 'LVT A Case Study Approach'. Lincoln Institute of Land Policy, working paper, 2001, p. 74. http://www.lincolninst.edu/pubs/100Land-Value-Taxation
10. Keall/Andelson, *Land Value Taxation...* p. 427, para. 2.
11. O'Regan, *Rating...* p. 79, para. 2.
12. Keall/Andelson, *Land Value taxation...* p. 423, para. 1.
13. Ibid. p. 420, para. 2.
14. http://www.sharechat.co.nz/article/07c29b10/opinion-the-rogernomics-revolution-20-years-on.html
15. New Zealand history: 'Goods and Services Tax Act comes into force,' Oct.1986, p. 1. http://www.nzhistory.net.nz/the-goods-and- service-tax-act-comes-into-force
16. Keall/Andelson, *Land value taxation...* p. 423, para. 4.
17. Keall, 'A Short History...' p. 3, para. 7.
18. Ibid. p. 3, para. 4.

19. McCluskey, Grimes & Timmins, 'Property Taxation in New Zealand'. Lincoln Institute of Land Policy, working paper, 2002, p. 19. para. 4, p. 20, para. 3 http://www.lincolninstdu/pubs/681Property- Taxation-in-New-Zealand

20. Keall, 'A Short History...' p. 3, para. 4

21. Barrett & Veal, 'Land Taxation...' p. 578, para. 2

22. Ibid, p. 577, para. 3

23. Magazines Today, Sir Roger Douglas: Bridget Gourlay interview, p.1, paras. 9 http://magazinestoday.co.nz/sir-roger-douglas/

Appendix 3: Case Study, The Pittsburgh Experience

1. Dan Sullivan,'Why Pittsburgh Real Estate Never Crashes' p. 4, para. 1 http://savingcommunities.org/places/us/pa/al/pgh/nevercrashes.html 2. Sullivan, 'Why Pittsburgh...' p. 4, para.

2. http://savingcommunities.org/places/us/pa/al/pgh/never crashes.html

3. Council of Georgist Organizations Conference, 2013. http://georgist.com/1-2013-february,announcement-update-from-cgo/

4. Ibid.

5. Pacific Standard on-line news magazine: 'This Land is Your Land' p.2, para. 2 https://psmag.com/news/this-land-is-your-land-3392

6. Sullivan, 'Why Pittsburgh...' p. 3, Para. 8

7. Percy R. Williams, 'Pennsylvania (its Experience With Land Value Taxation)', 1955 p. 5, para. 4, https://earthsharing.org/library/williams-percy_pennsylvania-1955/, reprinted from: *Land Value taxation Around the world,* first edition, 1955, editors Harry Gunniston Brown et al., Robert Shalkenbach Foundation.

8. John C. Rose, 'The Pittsburgh Graded Tax Plan', 1936, p. 6, para. 4 https://earthsharing.org/library/rose-john_pittsburgh-graded-tax-plan- 1936/?print=pdf

9. Percy R. Williams, 'The Graded Tax in the Redevelopment of Pittsburgh', 1963, p. 258, para. 3 https://www.jstor.org/stable/3484738?seq=1#page_scan_tab_contents

10. Ibid. p. 261, appendix A

11. Sullivan, 'Why Pittsburgh...' p. 5, para. 10

12. Wallace E. Oates & Robert M Schwab, 'The Impact of Urban Land Taxation: The Pittsburgh Experience', University of Maryland, 1996. p. 2, para. 2 https://www.jstor.org/stable/41789240?seq=1#pagescantabcontents

13. Percy R. Williams, *Pittsburgh's Experience with the Graded Tax Plan,* The American journal of Economics and Sociology, Vol. 22, No. 1, 1963, p. 158, para. 3

14. Mark Alan Hughes, 'Why so Little Georgism in America' Lincoln Institute of Land Policy working paper, 2005, abstract. p.4, para. 3

15. Hughes, 'Why so Little...' p. 8, para. 1

16. Rybeck/Andelson, *Land Value taxation Around the World,* p. 168, para. 4

17. Ibid. p. 169, para. 1

18. Hughes, "Why so Little...' p. 8 para. 3

19. Ibid. p. 8, para. 2

20. Ibid. p. 14, para. 2

21. Philly Record news website, 1st. July 2010. 'Land Value Tax: It's Worked to Cut Taxes, Boost Economics' p. 2 http://www.phillyrecord.com/2010/07/land-value-tax-its-worked-to- cut-taxes-boost-economies/

22. Next City. org, news website, 'Why Don't More Cities Tax Based on Value of Land Rather Than What You Put On It', Aug. 2013, p. 2 para. 8

23. Hughes, 'Why so Little...' p. 14, para. 2

24. Stephen B. Cord, Saving Communities, 'The 238 Report', Item 238, para. 4 http://savingcommunities.org/docs/cord.steven/238.html

25. Ibid. item 238, para. 6.

26. Flaherty Fardo, Attorneys at Law, 'Allegheny County Property Assessment, FAQ's', item 22, History, Jan. 9, 2002

ACKNOWLEDGEMENTS

This book was derived mainly from the material on my website, Land value tax Guide.com

In helping me to put the website together, some years ago, I owe my thanks to Mark Wadsworth, Brian Chance, Jesper Christensen, Dave Wetzel, Michael Hawes, Christine Arthur, Bob Rodens and Tony Dunbar, all of whom gave me the benefit of their expert knowledge, critical comment or encouragement in different ways.

For the book itself I would like to give my thanks to my friends Ann Randall and Victor Maynard for taking the time to proofread the draft text and especially to Jim Felici for his comprehensive and professional edit, which enabled me to avoid several pitfalls.

For their very helpful comments and suggestions on the draft manuscript, I'm indebted to several contributors to the *Land and Liberty* online magazine: The editor Joseph Milne, Andrew Purves (on Hong Kong and Singapore), Duncan Pickard (on agriculture), and Chris Wood for his detailed comments and an encouraging review. I would like to thank Carol Wilcox of the Labour Land Campaign for several helpful suggestions.

Also, I owe my thanks to Conall Boyle (on housing) and Bob Colenutt (author of *The Property Lobby*) for their helpful comments and Chris Waller for his supportive review.

INDEX

The suffix 'n' indicates references to notes.

Milton Keynes UK
Ingram Content Group UK Ltd.
UKHW011337120624
444118UK00042B/542